Thomas Wolfe's Albatross:

Race and Nationality in America

Paschal Reeves

Thomas Wolfe's Albatross:

Race and Nationality in America

UNIVERSITY OF GEORGIA PRESS · ATHENS

To my children
  Walter Paschal Reeves III
  Margaret Louise Reeves
With the hope that theirs may be a better America

Preface

Thirty years ago Thomas Wolfe died. Half of the six books on which his fame rests were already published, and the posthumous volumes appeared within three years. His books have not only remained in print but reprint editions, paperbacks, and translations have reached an ever–widening audience in America and abroad. The response of Wolfe's readers has resulted in a steady stream of literary criticism that is still expanding.

Many of these studies are focused on the man rather than his fiction. There are solid grounds for such an approach: Wolfe is certainly the most autobiographical of major American novelists and his intriguing personality continues to fascinate numerous readers. In creating his main protagonist as an *alter ego* he put more of himself into his books than did his contemporaries and consequently makes a greater personal impact on the reader. Hence the very nature of his writing calls for more understanding of the author for a proper evaluation of his work than is normally the case. For the most part, however, the special needs of scholarship resulting from Wolfe's autobiographical method have been met, and it is now necessary to give his work the judicious appraisal that is possible from the vantage point of three decades.

The present book is focused on Wolfe's fiction, the works he left to the world. Although their interrelatedness requires a holistic approach, their encyclopedic quality necessitates selectivity. While Wolfe formulated numerous plans and tested various themes, his ultimate goal was an epic portrayal of his native land, one that would reveal America in all its diversity and uniqueness. Central to this ambitious plan is the presentation of America's people with all their varieties of racial and national origin. He sought to accomplish this feat by endeavoring to project the autobiographical self into a generic American whose experience can encompass the full spectrum of peoples making up America and who can determine their backgrounds, mark their differences, probe their *ethos,* and assess their contributions to the American character. No comprehensive study has heretofore been made of this important aspect of Wolfe's writing, even though it is fundamental to an understanding of his total work and provides an essential key for determining his success or failure as an artist.

My study of Wolfe began long ago and the list of acknowledgements is correspondingly long. I am grateful to Paul Gitlin, Administrator of the Estate of Thomas Wolfe, and to William H. Bond for permission to quote from the unpublished writings in The Thomas Wolfe Collection of William B. Wisdom in the Harvard College Library.

Many librarians have assisted me in my research. The staff of the Houghton Library, especially Mr. Bond and Miss Carolyn Jakeman, have been most helpful. Miss Florence Blakely and Miss Mary Canada of the Duke University Library have given me aid far above and beyond the call of duty. The entire staff of the E. T. Roux Library of Florida Southern College was unfailingly helpful. William S. Powell of the University of North Carolina Library kindly supplied me with necessary information. I am most indebted, however, to Miss Myra Champion of the Pack Memorial Library, Asheville, for her invaluable assistance in finding answers to numerous questions that have arisen during my investigation.

A number of people have aided the writing of this book by furnishing specific information, making helpful suggestions, or contributing to my understanding of Wolfe and his milieu. Especially do I want to thank the following: Louis J. Budd, Francis W. Casey, William J. Cocke, Mrs. Elaine Westall Gould, Hans Helmcke, James S. Howell, Jr., Mr. and Mrs. Henry W. Jensen, Abraham I. Katsh, Klaus Lanzinger, William R. Linneman, Mr. and Mrs. George W. Lofquist, Bruce R. McElderry, Jr., Mrs. Beverly Hummel Ohler, Mr. and Mrs. Roscoe Parker, Norman Holmes Pearson, Louis D. Rubin, Jr., C. Richard Sanders, Miss Marion L. Starkey, Lionel Stevenson, Andrew Turnbull, Richard Walser, Robert Penn Warren, Floyd C. Watkins, Richard L.

Watson, Jr., the late Mabel Wolfe Wheaton, Thomas J. Wilson, Fred Wolfe, and Robert Lee Zimmerman.

For advice, released time for research, and financial assistance in the preparation of the final typescript I am grateful to the following colleagues at the University of Georgia: John O. Eidson, Robert A. McRorie, H. Boyd McWhorter, the late Edd Winfield Parks, and Robert H. West.

Brief portions of this book first appeared as articles in the *Explicator, Georgia Review, Modern Fiction Studies, South Atlantic Quarterly,* and *Southern Folklore Quarterly.* I wish to thank the editors for permission to reprint this material. For permission to reprint quotations from the published works of Thomas Wolfe I am grateful to Charles Scribner's Sons and to Harper & Row.

To three other friends I am particularly indebted. Arlin Turner was the first to encourage and guide me in my study of Wolfe. For his wise counsel through the years and his enlightening criticism of the manuscript in its earliest form, I am deeply grateful. Richard S. Kennedy has contributed greatly to my knowledge and understanding of Wolfe. Our joint labors on the Wolfe notebooks and the numerous ensuing discussions have been immeasurably beneficial to me. Another who has discussed Wolfe with me to my profit and shared valuable insights is C. Hugh Holman. I want to thank Mr. Kennedy and Mr. Holman for their critical readings of this book in manuscript and I hasten to absolve them from any blame for its faults.

My greatest debt is to my wife, Suzanne Smith Reeves. Constant in encouragement and indefatigable in assistance, she has truly made the writing of this book possible. There are no words to express fully my gratitude to her.

Paschal Reeves

Athens, Georgia
June, 1968

Contents

Thomas Wolfe's Albatross:

Race and Nationality in America

1 The Task:

'The Incomparable Substance of America'

In 1927 Thomas Wolfe wrote in his pocket notebook, "I'd rather write than be president," [1] and write he did, furiously and voluminously, until death stopped his hand in 1938. Driving himself mercilessly he wrote millions of words in his penciled scrawl in ledgers, notebooks, on yellow second sheets, memorandum pads, hotel stationery, menus, or whatever else was handy, and the six books of fiction which have been published from this huge output have elicited a wide range of responses. Although he was and still remains a controversial author, one point of agreement is that he gave the most comprehensive picture of his native land that has been achieved in fiction.

As a writer he was never reluctant to undertake the difficult or even the impossible. His reaction to a foreign restaurant is typical of his attitude. Once in a Budapest cafe he surveyed the midnight scene and wrote in his notebook, "The place is indescribable—therefore I shall try to describe it," and a two-page description follows.[2] It was this frame of mind which led him to attempt to portray the vast complexity of his native land on a scale which surpassed all of his contemporaries and was approached only by Dos Passos. Wolfe's fiction, whatever its shortcomings may be, would have merited the approval of Browning's Andrea del Sarto in at least one particular: his reach exceeded his grasp. The task which he attempted was as impossible as it was gargantuan. His "whole gigantic plan," as he reveals it in *The Story of a Novel*, "covered almost 150 years in history, demanded the action of more than 2000 characters, and would in its final design include almost every racial type and social class of American life." [3] Even though he realized that this desire was unattainable, it was ever the shining goal before him and to it he devoted unstintingly his energy and talent, and his accomplishment won high praise from William Faulkner: "Among his and my contemporaries, I rated Wolfe first because we had all failed but Wolfe had made the best failure because he had tried hardest to say the most." [4]

In his attempt to present American life with a totality that he had admired in Sherwood Anderson, Wolfe was an artist, selecting details, determining perspective, interpreting the whole; he was not merely a photographer of America. Neither was he a Gradgrind just after the facts; Wolfe the creative artist was striving for "something truer than facts—something distilled out of my experience and transmitted into a form of universal application." Thus his creative method was the distillation of experience, but that experience had to be Tom Wolfe's. He felt that in order to write about anything he must first make it a part of himself. Therefore, like Stephen Crane and Ernest Hemingway, he expended himself in quest for experience to provide the grist for his mill. Possessing an encyclopedic memory and the power of almost total recall, Wolfe became his own Boswell and his canon is freighted with what he calls "the enormous cargo of my memory."

This conscious quest and his storing up of experiential material antedates his career as a fiction writer. The day after he sailed from New York on his first trip to Europe (October 26, 1924) he wrote: "Today for the first time in my life, I am beginning a more or less methodical record of events which impinge on my own experience." [5] He continued this practice all his life and later drew upon these accumulated memories for his fictive material. Thus, no one can deny that what Wolfe produced is a highly personal record "of the whole web of life and of America." In fact, his total work constitutes an immense *Bildungsroman*. His method of rendering personal experience results in an unevenness of achievement that accounts for both his strength and weakness as a writer. The inclusion of the insignificant along with the important is a weakness that Wolfe himself recognized: "In my own life, there are some of the images that had no tangible importance or coherence and yet which, in the darkest blank and vacancy of memory, instantly and with no effort of my own, begin to burn there like a chain of shining lights." [6] He was, as he admitted to Scott Fitzgerald, an inveterate "putter-inner," and he often included the irrelevant for no other reason than it was luminous in his own memory. This indiscriminate use of experience has provoked some of the severest criticism that Wolfe has received, but it has also invested his writing with some of the qualities of the epic.

If Wolfe did not produce an American epic he at least burst the novel at its seams in the direction of the epic, and his failure is one of degree rather than of purpose. He constantly sought with a dogged tenacity to capture and to portray the essence of America in all its multiformity, complexity, and especially its distinctiveness. The seriousness of his purpose, the extraordinarily wide range of his experience, and the perceptive powers of his observation led him in his romantic odyssey to present a vivid panoramic view of American life, even though it may seem a highly individual and prejudicial one. The anachronistic quality that strikes a modern reader results largely from the fact that the pluralism in American society of Wolfe's own time is presented from a point of view more characteristic of the nineteenth century than of the twentieth.

Though Wolfe was town-born and spent the latter half of his life in large urban centers, he consistently identified himself with rural and pioneer America. He not only betrays this point of view often in his writing, but he ascribed it overtly to his autobiographical protagonist, George Webber, when he wrote of Webber's efforts to "devour" New York, "His own America was the America of the country man of the wilderness." This fictional affirmation is but a reiteration of what Wolfe had written to his mother six months after the publication of *Look Homeward, Angel:* "One half of me is great fields and mighty barns [of Pennsylvania], and one half of me is the great hills of North Carolina." It was through the eyes of a provincial rather than of a cosmopolite that Wolfe viewed his fellow countrymen.

Important as his provincial point of view is in bringing the urban dweller into focus, it is Wolfe's identification with pioneer America that brings into sharper relief the newer arrivals. His propensity for polarity led him to think of America not only as North and South or rural and urban, but also as "old" America and "new" America, and it was one of his chief sources of pride that he was numbered among the "old" Americans. And his long urban residence served to intensify his awareness of his background.

I am proud of my people, proud of my pioneer and mountaineer and Pennsylvania Dutch ancestry, and proud of the place I came from. . . . As I walk through the crowded and noisy streets of this immense city, and look at the dark swarthy faces of Jews, Italians, Greeks, and all the people of the New America that is roaring up around us here, I realize more keenly than ever that I come from the Old Americans—the people who settled the country, who fought its wars, who pushed westward.[7]

Wolfe's boast was not an idle one; his ancestors, both paternal and maternal, had arrived in America during Colonial times. His paternal grandfather, Jacob Wolf (the *e* was added by W. O. Wolfe), was probably descended from Palatinate Germans who reached Philadelphia in 1727, but the only certainty is that Jacob Wolf was born near York Springs, Pennsylvania, in 1806 or 1807. Wolfe's paternal grandmother, Eleanor Jane Heikes (or Heikus), was descended from colonists who arrived in Pennsylvania in 1720, but her genealogy had not been established prior to Wolfe's death. Wolfe knew with certainty only that his father's family were Pennsylvania German and had been resident in the York Springs vicinity for a century before his own birth. But his mother's family tree was established, and not only had her forebears arrived in America during Colonial times but some of them had resided in Western North Carolina since pre-Revolutionary days and were among the prominent families of the region. Consequently, it was his maternal ancestors who provided him with an indisputable pre-Revolutionary family tree, the basis for his fierce pride, and the source for George Webber's ancestry in *The Hills Beyond.*

Wolfe's mother was of English and Scotch-Irish descent. The Westalls, her father's people, came from England and were settled in Winchester, Virginia, before the Revolutionary War, and afterwards Thomas Westall, Wolfe's great-great-great grandfather, lived for a quarter-century in Western North Carolina before migrating to Texas in 1821. Mrs. Wolfe's mother was a Penland and her grandmother was a Patton, both notable Scotch-Irish families with distinguished pedigrees. Peter Penland served as a captain under George Washington in the French and Indian War, and Robert and Aaron Patton fought throughout the Revolution and took part in the battle of King's Mountain. Wolfe was a direct lineal descendant of all three; and his grandfather, Major Thomas Casey Westall, served in the Confederate Army under General Robert B. Vance.[8] Thus Wolfe could, with complete veracity, say that he came "from the old Americans—the people who settled the country, who fought its wars, who pushed westward."

His consciousness of his maternal relatives' long residence in Western North Carolina reveals itself in his writing. In a passage which was cut from *Of Time and the River* Wolfe describes a party which Eugene and Helen attended at the home of an Irish family which had recently moved to Altamont from Chicago. On his way home Eugene pondered the contrast between these gay newcomers and his own hillpeople; and Wolfe, writing first-person narrative, says, "it seemed to me that the earth, the hills, and my people who had lived among them for two hundred years had something secret, lonely, gaunt, and incommunicable in them, but that was yet wild and rich and strange." [9] His pioneer background was ever present in his mind and this realization was particularly acute when he was delineating characters who had more recently arrived in America.

Another factor which caused him to be very conscious of national origins, and one which he himself acknowledged, was the homogeneity of his native state. In his fictionalized essay on North Carolina, "The Men of Old Catawba," he notes this salient fact: "Although America is supposed by many of her cities [*sic*] to be a confusion of races, tongues, and peoples, as yet unwelded, there is perhaps nowhere in the world a more homogeneous population than that of Old Catawba." He further observes that North Carolina was relatively unaffected by the huge waves of immigration in the late nineteenth and early twentieth centuries and proceeds to give the national origins of its population as "English, German, and Scotch." In naming the three principal stocks which constituted the bulk of Tar Heels Wolfe was correct, and since they were also his own he felt an even greater identification with "Old Catawba." Wolfe, however, stresses the idea that these national stocks have fused to produce an indigenous American: "He is not a colonist, a settler, a transplanted European; during his three centuries there in the wilderness, he has become native to the immense and lonely land that he inhabits, . . . he has acquired a character, a tradition, and a history of his own."

The combination of his rural, pioneer point of view and his having grown up in a homogeneous region [10] resulted in a strong nativism that is everywhere apparent in his works. In freely expressing his prejudices Wolfe approaches H. L. Mencken, and despite the suggestions offered by Maxwell Perkins and the pruning done by Edward Aswell, Wolfe's writing remains the most uninhibited of major novelists of the twenties and thirties. As a representative of "old" America he is constantly alert to the "unwelded" elements in American life regardless of whether he encountered them infrequently, as he did in Asheville, or constantly, as he did in New York, and the resulting picture of the various "racial" types in his fiction was determined by his nativistic angle of vision.

Actually, "race" was for Wolfe a very general and loose term which he used for any group he wished to consider as a unit. At times he employs it in its ordinary sense, as when he writes about Negroes, but he invariably uses race in referring to the Jews, who are not a race in any technical sense though they are a supranational group. And by race he often means nationality too. Not only does he refer to English, Irish, German, French, and others as races, but when he calls the immigrant population of New York "the mongrel compost of a hundred races" he proceeds to list the countries of origin. Race also had other connotations to Wolfe; sometimes he applies it to geographical sections, occupations, or to such miscellaneous groupings as expatriates, but in spite of his seemingly inconsistent use of the word, it is clear from his total work that when he set out to include "almost every racial type" of American he meant both race, in its conventional denotation, and nationality. Any comprehensive treatment of America, and certainly one on the scale which Wolfe envisioned, must include discussion of race and nationality, and it is not his grand design but rather the execution of it that jolts the aesthetic sensibilities of modern readers, especially those who otherwise think of him as one of the authentic and lyrical voices of the twentieth century.

The twentieth century was but nine months old when Wolfe was born, and ideologically he owes more to the nineteenth than he does to the century of his birth. The shaping forces of nineteenth century concepts molded his formative years, and this heritage made him even closer intellectually and emotionally to the pioneer America whose homely values became his own early and, in some instances, his lasting loyalties. Among the many nineteenth-century ideas that he absorbed were its notions of racial superiority, exclusiveness, veneration for established tradition, distrust of unassimilated cultural patterns, and suspicion of urban values. Since these ideas found free expression in his fiction, no facet of his writing marks him so fundamentally a nineteenth-century man as does his treatment of race and nationality.

The importance of this aspect of his work, however, lies not only in the accurate rendering of the attitudes of the previous century, but also in the fact that here one can see the ideas of the nineteenth century struggling to become those of the twentieth, and even from this forge of experience comes the gleam of the twentieth century's great ideal, though as yet only partially attained—equality and brotherhood. Thus in his tortured prose picture of the America he knew, Thomas Wolfe has revealed some of his nation's anguish and travail in its own process of maturation.

2 The Negro:

'The Terrible Youth of an Ancient Race'

When Thomas Wolfe used the phrase "the terrible youth of an ancient race" in describing Eugene Gant's discoveries while prowling the Negro section of Altamont, he gave a succinct characterization of his own presentation of the Negro. The race he recognized as one whose origins were buried deep in unrecorded history, yet in his view the Negro maintained an eternal youth—a perpetual immaturity. He felt that three centuries in America had failed to obliterate the traits which the race had developed in countless ages in its original jungle habitat, and despite the civilizing forces brought upon it in America, had not begun to produce a maturity in any way comparable to that achieved by the white man. This concept of racial immaturity is everywhere apparent in Wolfe's depiction of the Negro.

To the casual reader it may seem that Wolfe practically ignored the Negro except for incidental slurring remarks about him and one account of a Negro slayer who ran amuck. Certainly there are none of the tribe of Harris's lovable Uncle Remus, nor notable ones like Mark Twain's Jim, nor stalwart ones like William Faulkner's Dilsey. Except for Dick Prosser there are no truly memorable ones at all, and there are no major Negro characters in Wolfe's books. Such an omission on the part of a Southern novelist writing about Southern life and seeking to portray the totality of that life—as well as the life of the nation as a whole—seems to be an almost deliberate attempt to ignore the Negro or at least to minimize him.

But Wolfe did not ignore the Negro nor did he make a conscious effort to minimize him out of proportion in the perspective which he viewed the Negro. Instead he wove the Negro into the background of his writing, only rarely allowing him to advance into full focus, but he nonetheless gave the Negro as honest an artistic treatment as he did himself, his family, his friends and acquaintances, or the stranger who crossed his path. The place of the Negro in the writing of Wolfe was determined by Wolfe's conception of the Negro's place in society. To Wolfe, as to Ellen Glasgow, the Negro was plainly a hewer of wood and drawer of water.

The Young Dramatist's View

Wolfe's earliest serious writing about the Negro is a fragment of an essay entitled "The Negro and the South's Economic Strength" which dates from his Chapel Hill or early Harvard days. It is probably a draft for a paper or theme which he wrote in one of his courses and relates to a statement he had recently read and to which he took exception.

> He refers to the negro as the race which has built up the South's economic strength and, without which, that strength "would topple to the ground." This is not true. The South would be stronger today economically and further advanced in the process of mechanical civilization had the negro never been brought within its borders. For this vast section, so generously endowed with every wealth of natural resources, has learned to place its dependence in the most primitive, the most indolent,—certainly the most inefficient laborer who ever leaned upon a spade. Had the South never been weighed down with this black millstone she would be infinitely farther advanced today in the [development, crossed out] exploration of her natural wealth.
>
> Lets give no misplaced sentiment to these noble Uncle Toms. A magic transportation back to the jungle (a dream in which most Southerners at one time or another indulge) would see completed in twenty years the cycle from savagery to savagery.[1]

The opinions which Wolfe expresses in this essay reflect the typical view held by most Southern intellectuals about 1920, and it was from this point of view that the young dramatist wrote his plays.

Wolfe dealt most directly with the Negro in the first substantial work, *Welcome to Our City*, in 1923. This not only is Wolfe's best

play, but remains the major treatment of race relations between
Negroes and whites in all his writing. Although the play was not
published until 1957,[2] it antedates the earliest of his prose fiction
(*Look Homeward, Angel* which he began writing in 1926) by
three full years, and thus gives a portrayal of the Negro as seen
through the eyes of the youthful playwright.

The original title of *Welcome to Our City*, written during
Wolfe's third year at Harvard, was "Niggertown," one which he
knew would engender criticism. In his prospectus, "A Scenario
For a Play in Four Acts/ To be Called Niggertown/ By/ Thomas
Wolfe," he wrote out a "Prefatory Statement" in which he de-
fends his choice of a title.

> I trust that there will be found nothing to provoke mirth in the
> title I have chosen for my play. Within the limits of that crude
> word are bound up too much human misery to cause any amuse-
> ment to thoughtful people who know the situation. It is a word
> that should not be printed: it should be stained on the page with
> sweat and blood.
>
> Gradually, I am becoming convinced that there can be no fair
> criticism of life in the South today which will not include in some
> tangible and distinctive way, the problem that has been created by
> the negro. The reasons for this conviction are manifold. I will give
> a few: First, the Southern negro comprises at least a third of the
> total population, possibly more than that. It is no unusual occur-
> rence in such states as Georgia, South Carolina, and Mississippi to
> enter towns where the negro population outnumbers the white.
> Indeed I believe that the negro population in these states would
> equal the white. In my own state, North Carolina, it is about a
> third.
>
> Second: The negro race has no moral or cultural background to
> give it spine. Let the optimistic call it lack of education, opportu-
> nity or what they will, but the fact remains that the race is incapa-
> ble of making the simplest ethical distinctions. It is not inconceiv-
> able [conceivable?] that a few years training can remedy this. The
> background from which a well-developed race must come is the
> product of centuries of slow and painful upbuilding, with the race
> consciousness and pride forever crystallizing and coming more and
> more into the visible foreground. The negro, even in those parts
> of the country where the laws technically put him on a social par
> with the white man, still clings to the pathetic delusion that his
> equality is to be maintained by a series of tawdry protests against
> segregation in schools, theatres, and moreover it is not true that
> education creates a moral sense. It sensitizes it perhaps, it gives it
> subtlety and penetration, but it cannot create it. A little reflection

will convince one that poverty, not ignorance, is the mother of crime.

If one of us, for instance, were asked to state his opinion on the probable conduct of a plodding laborer, industrious, and "law abiding," who, after fruitless attempts to obtain work, found himself and family at the very threshold of starvation, or of a brightly intelligent educated man who found himself and family in similar circumstances, but who was well informed on the laws governing distribution of wealth, and on Socialism—which, which of [breaks off]

[next sheet]

Indeed, a little reflection will prove that not ignorance but poverty is the mother of moral turpitude.

Education is unable to create the moral sense. It sensitizes and refines it, no doubt [3] [breaks off]

Before production, however, he did retitle the play in deference to the sensibilities of a New England audience, and *Welcome to Our City* was produced by the 47 Workshop on May 11 and 12, 1923.

He had gotten the idea for the play the previous summer during his visit to Asheville, where a real estate boom was in progress. The central plot of the play shows the efforts of a group of white real estate operators in Altamont to purchase an entire Negro section of the city, evict the Negroes, and rebuild it into a fashionable and expensive white residential area. When the Negroes resist eviction, feeling on both sides runs high and a race riot breaks out which the local National Guard quells with bloodshed. The dramatic situation is heightened by the fact that the Negro leader, a physician named Johnson, owns and lives in an old mansion which was the boyhood home of the white leader, Rutledge, and which Rutledge is extremely eager to obtain.

Despite its original title and the importance of Negroes to the central plot, the Negro was not the primary concern of the playwright. The theme of the play, as Wolfe expressed it in a letter to Margaret Roberts, is: "Greed, greed, greed—deliberate, crafty, motivated—masking under the guise of civic associations for municipal betterment." His chief interest is in the machinations of the Altamont Development Company to gain fat profits for itself under the guise of civic improvement in eliminating what the Secretary of the Altamont Board of Trade calls an "eyesore." Wolfe's choice in making this eyesore the Negro section of the city was based on a two-fold consideration. He could just as well have made the slum section one of poor mountain whites, such as "the

Doubleday Section" which he excoriates in *The Web and the Rock,* and which actually existed on the other side of Asheville. But he certainly realized that in making the slum dwellers Negro, in the clash of interests he was creating a black-white racial conflict that greatly intensified the dramatic situation. This was probably his chief reason in making the slum dwellers Negro; not for naught was Wolfe in his third year as a member of Professor Baker's 47 Workshop. However, it should be noted that in the physiography of Asheville, the slum section that abutted the business district, as depicted in the play, was a Negro section—the same one where he had delivered newspapers as a boy. Wolfe's later fictional fidelity to his geographic surroundings makes it impossible to rule out the second of these probable causes as a contributory factor in his choice.

It is the nature and scope of the play, rather than a concern for the Negro, which prompted Wolfe to give as extensive a presentation of Negroes as he does. Even at this time his literary vision was already the kaleidoscopic one which he was later to make famous in his novels. In writing to his cousin about his play he makes his motive quite clear: "My plan is concerned with giving a picture about a certain section of life, a certain civilization, a certain society. I am content with nothing but the whole picture, I am concerned with nothing else." This attempt to give the whole picture determines the place of the Negro in the play, for Wolfe vigorously denied that this was a "problem" play.

In the character of the Negro physician, Wolfe presents the emergence of the new Negro in the South at a mid-point in his development as a curiously hybrid personality. He has had the advantage of education and is a member of a privileged profession, yet vestiges of his primitive origin remain. In Dr. Johnson the "mad Negro laughter lurks forever behind his voice," a racial heritage apparently of his jungle savage ancestors, and although he chose to "act like a man," which brought his death, he does not quite die like one. The baying in his throat "like some giant mastiff" as he dies, indicates a sub-human, animal-like quality of racial taint that education, opportunity, achievement, and white blood have all failed to obliterate.

This depiction of Johnson as a man who made his peace with the whites and rose within the accepted framework to local eminence, then smashed the taboos and died for his pains, is sharpened by his contrast with Amos Todd. As Johnson is representative of the new Negro, so Amos is the symbol of the old; an Uncle Tom stereotype with "a very kindly face," he is the embodiment of

almost all the qualities which the South cherished in the good
old-fashioned darky. When Dr. Johnson rushes into Amos's shop
fleeing from the soldiers, Amos is killed as he looks out the window. The new Negro's comment on the death of the old is, "You
pore ole fool! Whut good's all your bowin' and scrapin' done
you?" Johnson, the rebellious doctor, and Amos, the faithful ar-
tisan, are the only two Negroes who meet death in the riot;
rebellious guilt and loyal innocence meet a common bloody fate
in the maintaining of the *status quo.*

The race riot, as such, is a very minor one. Wolfe did not
attempt to sensationalize the ending of his play with a riot of
major proportions. In the publication of the play, the editors of
Esquire capitalized on this element as "Race Riot in a Southern
Town." Actually, race riots at that time were, unfortunately,
rather common occurrences, nor were they confined only to the
South. In the three-year period from 1919 to 1921 serious race
riots occurred at Charleston, South Carolina; Chicago; Elaine,
Arkansas; Knoxville; Longview, Texas; Omaha; Washington,
D. C.; Duluth; Independence, Kansas; Ocoee, Florida; Springfield,
Ohio; and Tulsa.[4] The riot at the end of *Welcome to Our City* is
given as the inevitable outcome of naked greed trampling human
rights within the framework of racial tensions. Wolfe undoubtedly recognized it as good dramatic material, but it was also
necessary to the realistic treatment of such a situation in the year
1923, and Wolfe was nothing if not realistic.

In dealing with the Negro as a serious dramatic character at
this time Wolfe was near the forefront of this movement. Although Edward Sheldon, a Chicago-born playwright, began the
serious drama of the Negro in 1909 with his play *The Nigger,* it
was not until a decade later that this movement burst forth with
power upon the American stage. Eugene O'Neill, who wrote seven
plays dealing with the Negro between 1918 and 1924, brought the
movement to fruition when *The Emperor Jones* opened at the
Greenwich Village Playhouse in 1920. If Wolfe were influenced
by O'Neill, who had also been a member of Baker's 47 Workshop,
he was not imitative of him. O'Neill and Paul Green, Wolfe's
Chapel Hill classmate, were interested in the Negro for his intrinsic value as thematic material. Green's use of Negro material
throughout the early twenties culminated in his Pulitzer prize-win-
ning *In Abraham's Bosom* in 1927. But unlike O'Neill and Green,
Wolfe did not have an interest in the Negro as thematic material.
His persistent concern with "the whole picture" led him to depict
the Negro only as an integral part of that picture.[5] Undoubtedly

his Negroes, as the white characters in the play, are drawn from real life, from his own experience.

The Negro's Status in Society

The place of the Negro in society as delineated in the works of Wolfe with but two exceptions is that of servant and laborer. The Negro physician is one and the other is "the self-respecting negro, J. H. Jackson," who operated a fruit and vegetable stall in the market beneath the Altamont City Hall. Eugene Gant knew other substantial Negroes as a paperboy: "A good part of his subscription list was solidly founded among decent and laborious darkies —barbers, tailors, grocers, pharmacists, and ginghamed black housewives, who paid him promptly on a given day each week." But these more substantial Negroes remained just names on a subscription list and were not woven into the fabric of Wolfe's fiction.

This picture of the Negro as traced by Wolfe is that of an urban figure and no sharecroppers appear, for Wolfe was an urban writer despite his ambitious dream to portray "the whole web of life and of America." The rural areas are seen only in fleeting glimpses from the windows of a train while he was in transit from one urban oasis to another. Although he frequently used his great powers of description to paint word pictures of landscapes and pastoral scenes of lyric and haunting beauty, "life" in his writings is essentially urban. The sole rural Negro who appears in Wolfe's writing is one on the side of the road who was spotlighted briefly by the headlights of Luke's car as he was returning Eugene to Altamont after Eugene's release from jail in Blackstone, South Carolina. Thus, in the symbol that Wolfe employed in describing the expanding world of the growing Eugene, "a negro and his horse, together" the horse is certainly a drayhorse and not a plowhorse.

The Negro's place in society is even more strongly emphasized in Wolfe's description of the Negro community than it is in his presentation of the Negro's occupations. Wolfe's word for the Negro community was "Niggertown," and this is the term he almost invariably uses, whether in the context of describing the "hill-sprawled settlement" in Altamont or in contrasting a Paris bordello with vice in America. "Niggertown" is constantly set forth as a reeking slum of shabby dwellings, glutted with disease, strewn with filth, hot with lust, and infested with evil—over which hangs an aura of witch-magic and mystery. Not only is the social climate of such a community indicative of a racial immaturity but it is also one to impede seriously—if not prevent—the achieving of racial maturity. The inferior position of the Negro is illustrated by his economic and cultural poverty and by the degrading forces acting on his daily life.

Wolfe presents Eugene's boyish awareness of the Negro primarily as a sensory experience. Throughout his writing he exhibits great sensitivity for and facility in reproducing sensory impressions. Thus, when Eugene is sent by Eliza on an errand to "Niggertown," his impression of it is determined by the way in which it assails his senses—particularly his nostrils.

> Sometimes, when Eliza awoke to find her servants gone, he was sent down into Niggertown to capture a new one: in that city of rickets he searched into their fetid shacks, past the slow stench of little rills of mire and sewage, in fetid cellars, through all the rank labyrinth of the hill-sprawled settlement. He came, in the hot sealed dungeons of their rooms, to know the wild grace of their bodies, thrown upon a bed, their rich laughter, their smell of the jungle tropics stewed in with frying cookery and a boiling wash.[6]

"Niggertown" is a word with many connotations in Wolfe's writing—all of them bad. It meant something wicked, the location of brothels. When Eugene raised "his young goat-cry of desire" in apostrophe to a symbolic harlot, his words were, "Stand, Maya, by your opened door, denned in the jungle web of Niggertown." It meant something ominous. When Eliza told in "The Web of Earth" of the evidence that betrayed a man, the evidence was "that old red-clay Niggertown dust" on "his shoes and the bottoms of his trousers." It meant something repulsive. When George protested in his soul against the "little" errands for Aunt Maw, that protest became, "do not torture me . . . with the sunbaked clay and shambling rickets of black Niggertown!" It meant something sinister. When Wolfe sought to convey the ultimate, "It was dark as night, as evil as Niggertown, as vast as the elemental winds that howled down across the hills." But above all it meant the social sore emblematic of the Negro's place in society and of his racial immaturity.

This place is further underscored by Wolfe in his presentation of Negro-white relationships. The Negro is the ex-slave living in the land of his former owners, and neither—especially the white man—has forgotten the relationship that formerly existed. When Rutledge became incensed with Johnson's taunts, he exclaimed: "My father owned slaves, Sorrell, think of that!" This underlying fact is not always so evident in the overt actions of the characters themselves as it is evident in the overtones of the daily interplay between the two races as Wolfe reveals them. Since Wolfe in his novels and short pieces is writing about situations contemporary with his own life, for the most part, he makes no attempt to deal directly with slavery, except for the two satiric references to it in *Look Homeward, Angel.* However, in his play *Mannerhouse,* he does deal directly with slavery. In the Prologue he shows the subjugation of "savage black men" fresh from Africa. The relationships within the play are the traditional ones of master and slave.

Wolfe did give some thought to slavery for among his papers there exists a fragmentary essay on the South and slavery. In a four-page holograph manuscript he jotted down some random thoughts about slavery that include a verse attempt.

> The Southern nature has not changed very much, after all. The Southerner of Civil War days read Walter Scott and went to battle in the spirit of a crusader and a gallant—

> Cf Jeb Stuart

> The South in fiction has so often been colored with a melodramatic or romantic tinge—the Colonel, the old negro butler, the family pride, the heath of honesuckle [*sic*] etc—that when he comes north he finds he has a reputation to live up to, therefore if he's not careful you'd find him [part?] of the plot

> A Brief history of the Workshop
> Early beginnings   [Scratched out]
> Its grown from

> The mind has a natural inclination toward slavery: Were we less [unclassed?] we might be more honoring people—that we would be wiser I deny
>   SLAVERY
> Some men at the channel rail
> Some at heel and toe
> Some at sacked and [mirm?] grain
> Some at pleasure, some at pain
>   But
> Each somewhere, I trow
> Submit their [*sic*] selves to nine or fail
> Surrender
> [Submit, crossed out]
>   bow
> Surrender and [reverence, crossed out] low

Slavery is one of the great and essential facts of life. Slavery—our modern shibboleths of liberty fraternity and equality would be amusing if they were not so pathetic. Why has not someone paean-eyed slavery—I retract—Everyone has sung the praises of slavery but by using different words—

Religion is one of these words. For God's sake, be honest and call things by their proper name. Slavery is one of the great and [inspiring?] words,[7] [breaks off]

The ideas Wolfe expresses in this essay were not worked into his published writing *per se.* This essay may date from the *Mannerhouse* period, but it is probably later. Apparently Wolfe was working on a passage intended to be in a satiric vein as are his prose references to slavery in *Look Homeward, Angel.*

A sensitivity to Southern mores, however, is graphically shown by Eugene Gant's reaction in *Of Time and the River* when he was arrested. Eugene and three other young men were arrested in Blackstone, South Carolina, at the end of a wild, drunken ride. As Eugene was being put into a cell he saw that a young Negro was already in the cell. His resentment was instantaneous and violent; he furiously attacked the policemen and, cursing them roundly, endeavored to fight his way out of the cell door. In the ensuing melee the frightened Negro squirmed his way through the door, and Eugene then went resignedly back into the cell and was locked up. Eugene had just completed three years at Harvard, and his residence in the North had increased his tolerance but by no means had weakened his adherence to the mores of the South. On his way back to Altamont he said to Luke: "If it had happened in the North it would have been all right, but, by God, I don't believe they have any right in this State to put a white man in the same cell with a nigger!"

Miscegenation, on the other hand, is but briefly treated by Wolfe in his play. He does not moralize on it as a practice; he simply recognizes it as a fact. Although *Welcome to Our City* takes account of miscegenation, there is no searching examination of its tragic consequence such as O'Neill makes in *All God's Chillun Got Wings* and Green in *In Abraham's Bosom.* Of the nine named Negro characters in Wolfe's play, five are mulatto. Johnson, who obviously is proud of being a mulatto, denies to Rutledge that he is black. Johnson's daughter, Annie, vigorously denies that she is a Negro and, patting her hair as proof, tells Lee Rutledge, "Niggahs don't have straight hair like that, do they?" And the ambiguous relationship between the two races is vividly demonstrated by young Rutledge who sternly warns Annie never to speak to him on the street at the very time he is trying to seduce her.

The traditional Southern view that the infusion of white blood in a mixture raises the intellectual level is reflected by Rutledge. When he states that he has heard that Johnson is "a smart man," Sorrell replies, "For a Negro, yes." Rutledge quickly corrects Sorrell: "He's a mulatto. There's a difference." And this "difference" was one of the most firmly held of Southern tenets of the time.

In his novels Wolfe takes even less account of miscegenation. This standard theme of Southern novels is almost completely absent in Wolfe's; no Honoré Grandissime or Joe Christmas emerges on his pages. The presence of mulattoes testifies that miscegenation exists. Ella Corpening is a mulatto; so is Foxhall Edwards's cook. Judge Webster Tayloe, the wealthy lawyer, has a mulatto son. The passage about Judge Webster Tayloe (whom Wolfe calls Judge Webster Sondley in his manuscripts) is longer in the "O Lost" version since most of it was cut from *Look Homeward, Angel*. In the deleted portion Wolfe gives an account of a Negro woman in the dual role of cook and mistress, a role that the Negro in the South not infrequently fulfilled. This description is one of the earliest instances of Wolfe's interweaving of sex and food imagery to portray the primary womanly function as cook-mistress, the role in which he was later to cast Esther Jack. The mulatto's symbolic implications are further emphasized by the use of the "Dark Helen" refrain, one of Wolfe's favorite images which he elsewhere enlarges and applies to various themes —the South and Germany, among others.

> Leaving the music room he crossed a wide broad-boarded hall and entered the kitchen. The mother of his two sons, a tall powerfully molded negress of thirty-eight years, worked quietly over breakfast. His face bloomed with strange dark vitality as he looked at her. She made a great music to him: as he looked again at her sinuous cat body, the splendid depth of her breast, the great slope of her thighs from hip to knee, and the rich unblemished copper of her skin, he was sure once more that she was the most beautiful woman he had ever seen. Upon a grid she was lading thick clots of buckwheat batter four at a time, which she piled, when cooked, upon a smoking stack at her side. Meanwhile in a frying pan she spread out carefully wide streaky rashers of home cured bacon, keeping them limp and underdone, and weaving them skilfully through the texture of frying eggs which she turned and cooked, as he liked them best, hard.
>
> Dark Helen in my dark heart dreaming.[8]

As Wolfe continued to think about the relationship between the two races in the South he decided, by the oversimplification of which he was sometimes capable, that the crux of the matter was sex. In a passage cut from *Of Time and the River,* after a discussion of religion in the South, he proceeds to state his view of the "negro question."

> But if my real beliefs in other matters had become known, I would not have been condemned for them—I would have been lynched. The monster that I hated—that lorded over the South—was a sex monster. All of the powerful emotions—jealousy, hatred, rage, fear—that others had over God and evolution I felt over sex. The common end to all argument about sex—all unorthodox argument—was a reference to one's Mother and Sister.
>
> "How would you like *your* Mother or Sister to have been that?" Or
>
> "How would you like *your* Mother or Sister to be treated like that?"
>
> This put an end to the matter—no one had courage to say, "To hell with my mother and sister—let's get at the truth."
>
> The negro question is of course a sexual one. The Southerner likes the negro as long as he can keep him "in his place"—that is, in a kind of benevolent slavery, but he will not stand for his "putting on airs" or thinking he's "as good as a white man." This is the trouble: the Southerner fears that, so far as sexual potency is concerned, the negro is not only as good as a white man, but a great deal better. The lynching bees, and the occasional roasting parties in the public square, where the negro, accused of the usual offense, is stripped in the presence of white males, and the ladies of the town, castrated, and burned slowly in oil, is only a form of sexual sadism.
>
> And when the cadences of life are in our hands, when we can stop and start the pulses at will, let us lie down in gentle death for fifty thousand years, then born again, unwearied, let us reclothe those bones with life and love, and so go on forever.[9]

He was entirely correct in his assumption that the statement of any such view would have infuriated his fellow Southerners. To the Southerner of Wolfe's day this idea would have been considered the most despicable of heresies.

The above passage was written sometime between 1930 and 1934 after Wolfe had been away from the South a decade or more and viewed his native region from the perspective of prolonged Northern and European residence. Yet when his setting is the South he presents a realistic portrayal of his Southern characters with the typical attitudes he had encountered in his contemporaries.

In Negro-white relationships the place of the Negro in society is that of an inferior race.[10] He is the object of prejudice and is subjected to scorn, indignity, and even a patronizing affection. His behavior is judged by his white neighbors in accordance with his conformity to customs and traditions developed for him and imposed on him. He is treated as a member of a race that has not yet achieved maturity; he is still tainted by the onus of slavery.

Composite Characterization

Wolfe's principal method of characterization is portraiture, at which he is undeniably adept. His books, like a great art gallery, abound in portraits which vary all the way from huge, full-length, outsize ones down to tiny miniatures and with all graduations in between. Some are so extensive as to be book-length or even longer, like the towering figures of Eliza and old Gant which dominate the first two novels. But full, vibrant portraits are numerous: the loyal Helen, the tragic Ben, the pathetic Starwick, the inimitable Bascom Pentland, and the beloved Esther Jack are but a few. Others, by comparison to these full-length ones, are but thumbnail sketches, yet the reader feels he fully knows the person, whether it be Judge Bland of Libya Hill or The Microscopic Gentleman from Japan. And interspersed throughout are brief glimpses of the many captured only in passing—the miniatures of Wolfe—such as the panoramic gallery he presents in Eugene's walk through the town in *Look Homeward, Angel*. Much like Chaucer's, Wolfe's genius showed itself in portraiture.

All of these portraits, however, whether lengthy or brief, share a common quality; they step from the pages as real people, breathing the warm, moist air of life. They are not the static, two-dimensional pictures of a photographer, but are rather the three-dimensional portraits of a skillful artist to which has been added the fourth dimension, so characteristic of Wolfe—time. This artistic forte of Wolfe has been universally recognized.

In his treatment of the Negro, Wolfe does not follow his usual method of portraiture in that he does not present the Negro with the fullness with which he deals with many of his other background characters. For example, he frequently gives the others names, even those who flash briefly on his pages: the lone policeman eating a pre-dawn snack in Altamont's Uneeda Lunch is Big

Bill Merrick; a fellow roomer of Eugene Gant's at the Coulson's farm is Captain Nicholl; and the Italian elevator operator in the apartment building in New York where George Webber lived is Joe. One of the reasons for the obscurity of the Negro in Wolfe's works is that many of the Negro characters are anonymous. None of the servants at Dixieland or old Gant's Negro helpers is named. The Pullman porter who appears in both *Of Time and the River* and *You Can't Go Home Again* and for whom "one warms with friendship" is nameless, as is the Negro who is the night elevator operator in the apartment building where Joe is the day operator.

In the Chapel Hill sequence of "O Lost" Wolfe had a sketch of the old Negro janitor at the medical school, but it was not included in *Look Homeward, Angel*. The portrait of the janitor is a sympathetic one, but the old Negro is also nameless.

> Pickling in cellar vats of strong formaldehyde the bodies of eight men awaited their turn upon the tables of the medical school. They were all executed criminals: negroes who had been electrocuted at the State Penitentary in Sydney. When the students needed a new body for anatomy, an old negro janitor fished one from the vat. He was a benevolent old fellow with cotton whiskers, a good reverential slave, adoring his young masters who treated him well and generously. He was a devout and orthodox man. Sometimes he preached in a negro church on Sunday. His contacts with the lifeless engine of flesh never struck down his faith.
>
> The old man lived alone. His wife was dead. He had sons and daughters, but they had all married or gone away. One of them had been absent many years, and from whom he had never heard, he found in the pickling vat one day, dredging up from the abyss of crime and death a pattern of destiny as complete and terrible as that by which the prince who wived his mother once killed his father where the roads meet in the Phocian land.
>
> Then the old man put the body on a truck and mounted to the dissecting room.[11]

The named Negro characters are few indeed and are often completely irrelevant to the thread of the narrative. They are most numerous in *Look Homeward, Angel*, where there are only eleven—or possibly only ten: Tom Flack, hack-man; Uncle Thaddeus Evans, who died in the playhouse; Moses Andrews, who was murdered, Jefferson Flack, the murderer, and Miss Molly Fiske, their mutual mistress; J. H. Jackson, vegetable dealer; May Corpening; Annie, Mrs. Selborne's cook; and Ella Corpening. (It is likely that May Corpening and Ella Corpening are the same person—probably just a slip of Wolfe's pencil—since Corpening is his favorite name for a Negro prostitute; she is Essie Corpening in *Welcome to Our City*.) Of these, only two, Annie the cook and Ella Corpening, actually enter into the action of the narrative; the others are just sketched in passing. In *Of Time and the River* there are but three: Myrtis, Helen's "little nigger servant girl," "the nigger Jacken, the fruit and vegetable man," and Joe Corpening, hospital orderly. Two of these, Myrtis and Jacken (J. H. Jackson in *Look Homeward, Angel*), only flit across the page in one of Helen's insomnious musings. Joe Corpening's contribution is merely to assist Dr. McGuire out of the hospital and into Luke's car. *The Web and the Rock* has seven Negro characters: John Forman, the barber; Simpson Simms; Jenny Grubb, Mrs. Charles Montgomery Hopper's cook; James, the bootblack; Pansy Harris, the Shepperton's cook; Harris, her husband; and the one who is by all odds the most important of Wolfe's Negro characters, Dick Prosser. *You Can't Go Home Again* has but three: Carrie, who borrowed money from Judge Bland; Old Prove, who worked for Mark Joyner; and Portia, Foxhall Edwards's cook. Carrie enters the narrative very briefly; the other two not at all. The only two prominent Negroes who are named in Wolfe's published writing are Jack Johnson and Jesse Owens.

The characterization of the Negro in Wolfe's novels is largely as a composite figure and not as separate individuals. (The single exception to this statement is Dick Prosser who is discussed below.) This characterization of the composite Negro is the result of Wolfe's cumulative method, a portrayal by means of fragmentary details and widely-scattered references. The net result of this characterization is a portrayal of the Negro as an inferior and animal-like creature. Certain attributes and physical characteristics are singled out and emphasized by repetition. One of these is the voice, which is treated as a distinctive feature in the Negro. Sometimes it is comic, at others hearty, wailing, or howling, and though it may be rich in tonal quality, it is never well modulated or cultivated.

Wolfe does not portray the Negro without any redeeming virtues, but references to such traits are very rare. He may note some quality, such as composure, "the black mournful calm of the negress's face," or an attribute worthy of praise, such as devotion, but these rare references are as a rule made to individuals and are not intended as racial tributes. Though the Negro is not depicted as devoid of any good qualities, such touches are in extremely small proportion to those on the other side of the ledger.

In the light of this delineation of the Negro it is no wonder that
critics have taken Wolfe to task for his attitude. Leo Gurko's
comment on Wolfe is both typical and understandable: "He is
equally contemptuous toward Negroes, whom he seldom calls
anything but 'niggers.' At best they hardly qualify as human
beings." [12] But Wolfe's fidelity to his purpose in his portrayal of
America accounts in part for his depiction of the Negro. His
presentation of the Negro's place in society and his composite
characterization of the Negro is his attempt at objective realism,
tempered of course by his own artistic limitations, and in this
effort Wolfe accurately reflected the attitudes toward the Negro in
that segment of America with which he was most familiar.

A Note of Protest

Wolfe does depart from tradition in one significant particular
—he introduces a note of protest against maltreatment of the
Negro. This demurrer, almost entirely lacking in his earlier
works, is barely perceptible when it first appears but rises in
intensity and vigor until it becomes a full-voiced protest. When it
reaches a culmination in *You Can't Go Home Again* in the
scathing denunciation of Judge Bland's "business," Wolfe's protest becomes a slashing attack on a condition in the South which
had helped to keep the Negro in economic bondage.

The principal difference between Eugene Gant and George
Webber in regard to the Negro is that there enters into Webber
this note of protest which is not present in Gant. In his first two
novels Wolfe presents the Negro as Eugene sees him, encounters
him, and reacts to him. The Negro is not treated for any intrinsic
literary value he may have; he is there simply because he is
necessary in showing the whole range of Eugene's experiences.
Like the town square or the family across the street the Negro is
part of Altamont and thus becomes a portion of Eugene's total
experience. But there is no note of protest raised in his behalf. His
status in society is accepted as the natural role for him, and his
community is tolerated as a necessary evil. His plight elicits very
little sympathy from Eugene and certainly no protest. True, there
are two instances in *Look Homeward, Angel* where slavery is
mildly satirized, but slavery as an institution had been dead
thirty-five years when Eugene (and Wolfe) was born. Protesting
slavery then was flogging a dead horse. Against the contemporary
conditions which enmeshed the Negro, Eugene protested not in
the slightest.

The place where one might naturally expect to encounter any protest by Wolfe in the Negro's behalf is *Welcome to Our City*. The central plot afforded him an excellent opportunity to render a protest had he been so inclined. But at twenty-two he was not so minded. Thus, in his plays—as is true in his first two novels—he makes no protest against the conditions which confronted the contemporary Negro.

In his posthumous novels Wolfe does give to the George Webber story a note of protest against the maltreatment of the Negro, but the first published note of protest is found in "The Face of War"—initially published in *Modern Monthly* for June 1935. In the first of "four moments from the face of war" a Negro at Langley Field is "beaten to a bloody pulp" by a "slouchy, shambling figure of a Southern white—a gang boss or an overseer." Wolfe does not articulate his protest, but he does make it clear to the reader that in this presentation of a "nausea of horror" his sympathies are with the victim and that the assailant and the office clerk merit his contempt. Certainly his handling of the incident in the context of this piece is even more than an effort to show the brutality and sordidness resulting from war; it marks the first time in print that Wolfe is found on the black man's side in the continual struggle between the races. Notable, too, in the incident is the fact that Wolfe does not attempt to assay the innocence or the guilt of the Negro. Whatever might be the implications of "talking back," it is the treatment the Negro receives that is resented and—by the nature of its presentation—is protested.

Early in *The Web and the Rock* Wolfe goes a step farther and depicts the treatment of the Negro as the suffering of the innocent. This portrayal is occasioned by the dogfight between the Potterhams' bulldog and the mastiff belonging to Simpson Simms, symbolically named Storm. The Negro's dog is the object of an unprovoked attack by the Potterhams' bulldog. Thus, not only is Simms innocent but even his dog is innocent. When Storm reacts quickly and kills the offending bulldog, the stage is then set: a white man's dog has been killed by a Negro's. The roles just played by the dogs are reenacted by their owners. Potterham denounces the Negro's dog to the policeman, who takes notes in his book and tells Simms to appear in court. This theme of the Negro as innocent sufferer, briefly sketched in this episode, is made more evident in the Dick Prosser story when Dick is assaulted by the drunken Lon Pilcher after the accident for which Pilcher solely is to blame.

Wolfe was well aware of the fact that the Negro constituted approximately one-third of the population of his native state; his delight in statistics of all kinds made them a life-long hobby. In writing about the State of Old Catawba he noted that "Upon this area, which is a little smaller than the combined areas of England and Wales, there live three million people, of whom the third part are black." He was also cognizant of the fact that this black third was disfranchised and denied—to a large extent—the opportunity for higher education. Against this disfranchisement and denial of higher education Wolfe also protested. His criticism of this violation of the Negro's "civil rights"—a term Wolfe nowhere used—is found in the context of a larger indictment of Pine Rock College for its failure to provide the educated and inspired leadership to aid in eliminating the social, economic, and political ills of the South.

> In fact, in spite of all this high-sounding talk about "service," "ideals of leadership," and "democracy," one could not see that it made much actual difference in the way things were. Children still worked fourteen hours a day in the cotton mills of the state. Tens of thousands of men and women and children were born, suffered, lived, and died in damnable poverty, bondage, and the exploitation of the tenant farm. *One million black inhabitants of the state, about a third of the entire population, were still denied the rights of free suffrage*—even though the "second greatest man since Jesus Christ" frequently declared that that right was one of the proudest triumphs of Anglo-Saxon law, and of the nation's own great Constitution. *One million black inhabitants of the state were denied the right to the blessings of the higher education*—although "the second greatest man since Jesus Christ" often declared that it was for this ideal that Pine Rock College lived and had its being, and that the right of education would be denied to no fit person at old Pine Rock, "regardless of creed, color, race, or other distinction of any kind whatsoever." In spite of the sounding phrases, the idealism, the martyred look, the inspired assurances, and all the rest of it, life went on according to the old formula, and in the old way, pretty much as it had always done.[13] (Italics mine.)

The recognition of these facts in such a context constitutes a protest in itself, and the expression of such views indicates that Wolfe—writing as a Southerner—was in advance of his time.

Wolfe's most vigorous protest in behalf of the Negro is that against the financial exploitation of the Negro. He touches upon this in *The Web and the Rock* when George reasons that Aunt Maw's cook had quit "because you failed to pay the poor wench on Saturday night the three dollars which is her princely emolument for fourteen hours a day of sweaty drudgery seven days a week." This underpayment for such long hours rankles in George's mind when he objects to being sent to find a replacement. But it is the loan-shark who devours the meager resources of the Negro that aroused Wolfe to utter his strongest denunciation against the maltreatment of the Negro. In the *Saurday Evening Post* version of "The Child by Tiger" he brands the loathsome Ben Pounders as "the collector of usurious lendings to the blacks." In the *Post* version it is Pounders who boasts he had gotten the first shot at Dick Prosser; in the novel version the braggart is unnamed. However, when Wolfe revised "The Child by Tiger" for *The Web and the Rock* he changed Pounder's name to Clyde Early and made his denunciation of Early even more vociferous.

> It was Clyde Early, Clyde Early of the ferret face, furtive and uneasy eye, Clyde Early of the mongrel mouth, the wiry muscles of the jaw, Clyde Early, Dinwood [later changed to Rumford] Bland's collector and chief agent, the overseer of Dinwood Bland's usurious lendings to the blacks, Bland's nigger hunter, Bland's scourge and whip, Bland's rattlesnake. And now Clyde Early boasted of another triumph. He was the proud possessor of another scalp.[14]

And in *You Can't Go Home Again* he excoriates Judge Bland for his "business," all of which "was derived from the Negro population of the town, and of this business the principal item was usury."

Judge Bland is the blind lawyer whose "legal skill and knowledge had been used more for the purpose of circumventing the law and defeating justice than in maintaining them." He operated a second-hand furniture "store" with a "mountainous heap of ill-smelling junk . . . taken as brutal tribute" from Negroes. This store was "nothing but a blind for his illegal transactions with the Negroes." Judge Bland would lend them money and thereafter extract exorbitant interest for the loan, *five* per cent *per week:* "The interest was payable weekly, every Saturday night. On a ten-dollar loan Judge Bland extracted interest of fifty cents a week; on a twenty-dollar loan, interest of a dollar a week; and so on." Judge Bland did not want the principal repaid, but only that the Negroes keep up the interest out of their small wages which "if they were men, might not be more than five or six dollars a week, and if they were women—cooks or house-servants in town—might be only three or four dollars."

> Judge Bland had on his books the names of Negroes who had paid him fifty cents or a dollar a week over a period of years, on an original loan of ten or twenty dollars. Many of these poor and ignorant people were unable to comprehend what had happened to them. They could only feel mournfully, dumbly, with the slave-like submissiveness of their whole training and conditioning, that at some time in the distant past they had got their money, spent it, and had their fling, and that now they must pay perpetual tribute for that privilege.[15]

Wolfe then proceeds to attack this practice of "unscrupulous white men all over the South" and the complicity of police injustice which condoned it. In the vehemence of this attack he approaches the intensity of his slashing comments on other social ills in America not so directly related to the Negro. Here the Negro is treated with a sympathy and an understanding he does not always receive from Wolfe. This salvo in *You Can't Go Home Again* is the strongest one he fired in a growing note of protest against the maltreatment of the Negro in his later work, some of which remains unpublished.

In *You Can't Go Home Again* Wolfe gives what to him is "The Promise of America": "to every man his chance—to every man, regardless of his birth, his shining, golden opportunity—to every man the right to live, to work, to be himself, and to become whatever thing his manhood and his vision can combine to make him." In this context he traces the progress of the Negro.

> Here, as you pass through the brutal sprawl, the twenty miles of rails and rickets, of the South Chicago slums—here, in an unpainted shack, is a Negro boy, and, seeker, he is burning in the night. Behind him is a memory of the cotton fields, the flat and mournful pineland barrens of the lost and buried South, and at the fringes of the pine another nigger shack, with mammy and eleven little niggers. Farther still behind, the slave-driver's whip, the slave ship, and, far off, the jungle dirge of Africa. And before him, what? A roped-in ring, a blaze of lights, across from him a white champion; the bell, the opening, and all around the vast sea-roaring of the crowd. Then the lightning feint and stroke, the black panther's paw—the hot, rotating presses, and the rivers of sheeted print! O seeker, where is the slave ship now? [16]

In this account of the Negro's progress in America Wolfe sees the Negro's pursuit of fame as achieved primarily through physical prowess and skill, such as boxing, in an episode reminiscent of the career of Joe Louis—the reigning heavyweight champion during the last year and three months of Wolfe's life. It is significant, then, that the only two actual Negroes of prominence who are mentioned in Wolfe's books—Jack Johnson and Jesse Owens— are both athletes.

Aside from his remarks about disfranchisement and denial of higher education there is no other evidence that Wolfe had in mind institutional change; he was not a reformer like George W. Cable. Perhaps this is only a manifestation of Wolfe's humanitarianism, a desire for more humane treatment of all the oppressed— the Negro in the South or the Jew in Germany. Whatever his reasoning may have been, Wolfe recognized something amiss in the total pattern of the South and made a protest against the maltreatment of the Negro which was growing more audible at the time of his death.

The Tiger and the Child

The sole instance in any of his novels where Wolfe devotes an entire chapter to a Negro is "The Child by Tiger" in *The Web and the Rock*. This is the story of Dick Prosser, undeniably the most important and most memorable of Wolfe's Negro characters. Since this story was completed in the spring of 1937—just a little over a year before his death—it is some of his most mature writing on the Negro and merits special scrutiny.

"The Child by Tiger" was first published as a short story in the *Saturday Evening Post* of September 11, 1937. The magazine story is a first-person narrative of the author's recollections of the Dick Prosser affair which is purported to have happened twenty-five years previously. The narrator—simply "I" in the story—recalls the harrowing experiences of Prosser, the faithful family retainer who ran amuck and committed multiple, indiscriminate murder before he was hunted down by a posse and killed.

This story was originally written much earlier in Wolfe's career. In a letter from Montreux, Switzerland, Wolfe wrote Maxwell Perkins in 1930 about the book on which he was then working (and which was published five years later as *Of Time and the River*) and mentions that "in the chapter called 'The Congo,' [17] the wandering negro who goes crazy and kills people and is finally killed by the posse as he crosses a creek." Much of the material on which Wolfe was working at that time, however, never got into the final draft of *Of Time and the River*. While he was in Germany in 1930 he had listed the story as a project in his notebook as " 'Nigger Dick'—the coon who is hunted by the posse." [18] This story continued to interest him and in 1933 he included it in a list of scenes for his writing as "The Nigger Killer." [19] Thus by the time he got around to rewriting the story in 1937 it had undergone a long gestation period in his mind, and benefited from his increased concern with man's inhumanity to man which grew out of his experiences in Nazi Germany in 1936. And the short story became a chapter of the novel with only minor changes.

The raw material for this story, as in so much else that he wrote, Wolfe took directly from life. The plot was ready-made for him by actual happenings in Asheville in November 1906 when Will Harris, a Negro, ran amuck and killed five men and was himself finally run down by a posse and killed. The following account of the actual events is taken from the issues of the *Asheville Citizen* of November 14, 15, and 16, 1906.[20]

On Tuesday, November 13, 1906, a Negro man purchased a .303 calibre Savage rifle and twenty cartridges from the shop of pawnbroker Harry Finklestein in Asheville. This man was later identified as Will Harris of Charlotte. About midnight Harris was in the basement room of a house on Valley Street occupied by Toney Johnson, a Negro, and "the woman with whom he stayed," identified only as Pearl. An altercation broke out between Harris and Johnson, and Johnson ran to police headquarters and reported the incident after Harris had attempted to shoot him with the rifle. Julia Thomas, a Negro woman who lived above Pearl, heard the commotion and went downstairs to investigate. She opened the door and saw Harris, the rifle across his knees, sitting with Pearl. As she started to enter the room Harris pointed the gun at her and she fled.

About this time Captain Page of the police, to whom the incident had been reported, and Patrolman Charles R. Blackstock arrived and attempted to arrest Harris. Harris shot Blackstock, killing him at once, and wounded Captain Page in the right arm. Harris then fled up Valley Street. He shot a young Negro man named Walter Corpening, alias "Jakko," on Valley Street, and Corpening crawled into an alley and died. (His body was not found until the following morning, so that his death was not known at the time the alarm for Harris was first given.) As Harris turned into Eagle Street he saw Benjamin F. Addison, an old Negro who had a little grocery store at 53 Eagle Street, standing in the door of his store. Harris shot Addison and killed him instantly, the bullet passing through the right eye and out the back of his head. Farther up Eagle Street Tom Neil, a Negro, turned around to see what was happening. Harris shot him in the groin, and Neil staggered into a stairway and fell. He was operated on the following day but later died as a result of the wound. When Harris reached South Main Street (now called Biltmore Avenue) he turned and walked toward Pack Square—the center of Asheville—shooting at everyone in sight. As he passed the Laurel Valley saloon, George W. Jackson, the Negro bartender, came out. Harris fired at Jackson, but the bullet went through Jackson's trousers and he fled unhurt. As Harris neared Pack Square, Patrolman J. W. Bailey stationed himself behind a telephone post and fired at the approaching Harris three times. Harris dropped on one knee and shot at Bailey. The bullet passed through the telephone post into Bailey's mouth and lodged in his brain. Death was almost instantaneous.

After killing Bailey, Harris turned around and went back down South Main Street and headed toward Biltmore. He shot at everyone who appeared. As he passed the British-American Club, Spears Reynolds shot at Harris with a pistol. Harris turned and fired at Reynolds, barely missing him, and went on down the street. A woman who looked out of a hotel window also became a target, but the bullet struck just below the window sill. Harris fired at a man in the Swannanoa Hotel just as the man turned out a light, and the bullet hit the wall. Harris continued on down South Main Street and disappeared into the night.

As soon as the extent of Harris's wild rampage became known, Chief of Police Bernard had the city fire bell rung as a riot call. A large crowd quickly gathered in Pack Square and demanded arms to follow Harris. Harry Finklestein, the pawnbroker who had sold the rifle to Harris the previous day, distributed all the weapons that he had in his shop. But this did not arm all who desired arms, and the crowd repeatedly requested Chief Bernard to break into the Asheville Hardware Company and distribute the weapons there. He finally consented and did so. While this distribution was in progress, the manager of the hardware store, Claybrook James, arrived and consented to it. Posses were hastily organized and sent off in various directions to look for Harris, but the search that night proved fruitless, although bloodhounds had been brought from Tryon to aid in the search.

Wednesday, November 14, 1906, was probably the most exciting day Asheville had known since North Carolina seceded from the Union. Indeed, the newspaper headline proclaimed:

"ASHEVILLE STIRRED TO ITS DEPTHS PASSES THE MOST EXCITING DAY IN ITS HISTORY." The search for Will Harris went on furiously. Armed men were everywhere, and the surrounding countryside was also in arms. Snow fell all day, but it deterred no one. Police headquarters was filled with people, false rumors were rampant, and posses were constantly being dispatched to surrounding communities where the fugitive was variously reported to have been seen. Telephone and telegraph lines hummed. All trains were searched and carried armed guards. Every Negro home in Asheville was searched. Rewards, from both the city treasury and public subscription, rose to more than a thousand dollars. Excitement remained at fever pitch; the search was pressed relentlessly, but the day passed and Harris was not found.

The next morning Harris was sighted near Fletcher, North Carolina, where he had spent the night in a barn. Word was flashed to Asheville and posses were dispatched by horseback and train. Later in the day Harris was surrounded in Blake's woods by about fifty men, none of whom was injured in the exchange of shots. After Harris had exhausted his ammunition he went down under a fusillade of shots from the posse. His body was then put in a wagon and returned to Asheville.

Crowds of people streamed out from Biltmore to meet the posse with the body, and when it reached Asheville it was met by huge crowds massed in every direction. It was with great difficulty that the body was finally taken to Hare, Bard and Company, undertakers. So great was the clamor of the unmanageable crowd to see the body that Coroner E. R. Morris finally directed the Sheriff to place the body in the window for the crowd to view. The riddled body, with one shoe missing, was then viewed by the vast crowd.

At the time Will Harris went on this murderous rampage Wolfe was six years old. But he could hardly have been unaware of what was happening at the time. Whether he actually saw the body of Harris is uncertain, but it is entirely possible that he did. The indication seems to be that he may have; at least he wrote in another of his books also that Webber saw Prosser's body. In *You Can't Go Home Again* Wolfe describes the capture of "Fuss-and-Fidget," the Jew who is attempting to escape from Nazi Germany. In commenting on the capture Wolfe writes:

> This is the tragedy of man's cruelty and his lust for pain—the tragic weakness which corrupts him, which he loathes, but which he cannot cure. As a child, George had seen it on the faces of men standing before the window of a shabby little undertaker's place,

looking at the bloody, riddled carcass of a Negro which the mob had caught and killed.[21]

Patrolman Blackstock lived at 40 Charlotte Street, around the corner from Wolfe's father's home on Woodfin Street, and had four children. It is likely that Wolfe knew the children and he may have known Blackstock. He seems also to have known Bailey for he refers to Bailey by his real name in *Of Time and the River*. In describing the "look" on the faces of the people Eugene saw in Oxford, England, Wolfe recalls:

> It was a look round, full, ruddy, and serene in its good-nature and had more openness and mellow humor in it than Eugene had found in the faces of the people in New England. It was more like the look of country people and small-town people in the South. Sometimes it had the open tranquil ruddiness, the bovine and self-satisfied good humor of his uncle, Crockett Pentland, and sometimes it was like Mr. Bailey, the policeman, whom the negro killed one winter's night, when snow was on the ground and all the bells began to ring.[22]

The strongest evidence, however, is what Wolfe wrote in his Autobiographical Outline. Among his recollections of childhood he included the Harris episode: "The snowy night when the negro killer came to town—He got five, including Mr. Bailey of the police—Mr. Bailey lived on Vance Street [23]—the hole through the telephone pole and the chip off the monument—The posse riddled him with holes." [24] Every boy in Asheville probably poked his finger into that hole in the telephone pole, and young Tom Wolfe may well have been one of them.

While the impressions of a six-year-old do not always last to adult life, one would be extremely reluctant to say that a person —especially one with such a phenomenal memory as Wolfe—did not actually remember such a dramatic event from his childhood. But more important, whether he remembered it or not, is the fact that during his childhood and youth he undoubtedly heard the story repeated many, many times, perhaps by eyewitnesses and participants, for discussions and speculations about it took place among the citizens of Asheville for years. In later years Wolfe's newspaper route covered a part of the section where these events took place, and he may have mused about them as he walked the same streets where Will Harris once shed the blood of both blacks and whites.

The foregoing details of the actual happenings, when compared with his fictional treatment of them, shed light on Wolfe's creative process. On the surface the story of Dick Prosser is remarkably like the actual happening—so much so, in fact, as to make one wonder whether Wolfe consulted the newspaper files before he wrote the final fictional version. He had been in Asheville in the spring of 1937 and could have done so. But it seems more likely that the great similarity is due to Wolfe's remarkable memory and his established practice of taking his material directly from life.

It is obvious that the basic plot pattern of the story was lifted bodily from the actual event. Many of the details of the two also coincide: the season of the year (October in the story, November in reality); snow was falling in both instances; the city was alarmed by the ringing of the fire bell; Harris dropped on one knee to shoot through a telephone pole and kill Patrolman Bailey, Prosser did likewise to slay Officer Chapman; both men had been drinking—police later found "the remnants of a gallon jug of raw corn whiskey" after Prosser's mad fling, and a "half-emptied bottle of liquor" was found by a newspaper reporter after Harris's. The list could be extended, but it is sufficient to demonstrate the similarity even of detail.

To say that Dick Prosser *was* Will Harris, however, is to ignore the creative ability of Wolfe and to miss the main clue to his method. Prosser is a good deal more than Harris, although Harris must be conceded to be the skeleton on which Prosser was fashioned. The central feature of Wolfe's creative process was synthesis. Even though he took his characters from life, he fused them together in such a way as to produce a character new in depth, new in meaning, and new in symbolism—even though the original model is perhaps still recognizable. He himself admitted as much when he wrote in *The Story of a Novel:* "I added that Dr. Johnson had remarked that a man might turn over half the volumes in his library to make a single book, and that in a similar way, a novelist might turn over half the characters in his native town to make a single figure for his novel." Prosser represents the fusion of various Negroes that Wolfe had known or known about.

When the story was published in the *Saturday Evening Post* long-time residents of Asheville thought that they detected at least three real-life counterparts of the composite Prosser. One was Harris, of course. Another was an old Negro janitor at the Bingham School who was greatly beloved and constantly followed about by the students. The third was a Bible-reading chauffeur who had long served one of the local families and lived in a room in their basement.[25] Such conjectures may well be correct. Wolfe probably knew, or at least knew about, the latter two, but, in any event, they were representative types which were fairly common and which he certainly would have encountered in his youth.

The artistry of Wolfe shows clearly in the contrast between Harris and Prosser, and the metamorphosis that Harris underwent to become Prosser. As a result of Wolfe's synthesis, Prosser emerges as a greatly enriched figure able to play the central role in the action of the story and also to become the symbol of his race which Wolfe evidently intended him to be. Will Harris was a transient and had not been in Asheville long when he went on his mad spree of murder. Dick Prosser, though a relative newcomer to the town, had sought and found employment and had established himself as a trusted family servant. Nothing was known of Harris's activities in Asheville except his purchase of the high-powered rifle, although it was learned that two years previously he had broken out of the penitentiary where he was serving twenty years for burglary and arson, and that he had killed several men and had been outlawed by both the State of North Carolina and Mecklenburg County. Prosser was a model of the conduct expected of Negro servants by the white citizenry of Asheville of that day. Moreover, he was a devout man: "He was deeply religious and went to church three times a week." He read his Bible every night, believed "de Armageddon day's a-comin'," and sang hymns while he worked. Furthermore, he suffered innocently at the hands of an angry white man when he was assailed by the drunken driver after an accident. He suffered in silence and did not attempt retaliation. Prosser, the loyal family servant and army veteran, was a far different man from Harris, the desperado.

The increase in the number of victims of Prosser may have been made for dramatic and symbolic reasons but probably results partly from Wolfe's tendency to exaggerate. Harris killed five men, the two policemen and three members of his own race. Wolfe has Prosser slay nine men, two of whom were Negroes and the other seven whites. This increase in the number of victims heightens the dramatic element in the story—especially in the chase. The symbolic implications of it will be discussed later.

The presentation of the Negro in "The Child by Tiger" is in keeping with the traditional Southern attitude of the time. Wolfe accomplishes this by his use of diction, implication, and insinuation. ("Niggertown" is presented in the same light as is discussed above.) Standards of social and personal morality among Negroes were lower—or at least more open—than among whites. Liaisons without legal sanction were common and were accepted so that the Asheville newspaper on its front page merely noted of Toney Johnson, "Urged on by the woman with whom he stays." Wolfe reflected this attitude in his statement, "Adultery among negroes was assumed." Use of the term "wench" to describe Pansy Harris indicates that she was a woman of loose morals. Implications of the economic conditions among Negroes may be drawn from "Pansy Harris's shack" and "raw corn whiskey." The typical Southern belief that the Negro was less of a human being and more of an animal than the white man is subtly insinuated in the reference to Dick Prosser's "great black paw." Thus, Wolfe here, too, follows Southern convention.

In dealing with the death of Dick Prosser, however, Wolfe departs from tradition, for he treats it as a lynching and here again the note of protest enters. Actually, the mad murderer's death is not a lynching as that term is usually employed. He was a fugitive from justice, and his pursuers were deputized and charged to capture him dead or alive. Furthermore, he was armed and shooting at the posse. But the white men venting their fury on the black man's dead body, the triumphal return, and the display of the mutilated carcass are elements of lynching that Wolfe chose to accentuate and by implication to protest. This is not the first time he was concerned with lynching. When Eugene was a student at Pulpit Hill he felt that the "education" he was receiving was too far removed from coming to grips with the issues of the day, one of which was "lynching bees and black barbecue parties." In *The Web and the Rock* in his comparison of South Carolina and Old Catawba Wolfe describes the way "they go out to lynch a nigger" in South Carolina. His description indicates a strong distaste for lynching, but his protest is weakened by his purpose, the disparagement of South Carolina. But in the death of Dick Prosser, by his very handling of the narrative—in spite of Dick's guilt and mad-dog tactics—Wolfe seems, like Nebraska Crane, to spit contemptuously at the whole bloody business of lynching. Here the protest is unmistakable.

Conventional enough, too, are the elements of the plot: the murders, the chase by bloodhounds and posse, the riddling of the body with bullets, and the display of the body as a trophy of the hunt. What keeps Dick Prosser, however, from being simply the stereotyped figure of a tragic protagonist, is not the aura of mystery with which Wolfe surrounds him or the ferocity of Prosser's actions, but rather it is Wolfe's use of Prosser not as an archetype but as a symbol of his race.

Wolfe's mind, like Hawthorne's, naturally perceived people

and events as symbols, though perhaps not to the same degree that Hawthorne did. Only in babyhood was Eugene "in agony because he was poverty-striken in symbols," and he soon outgrew the condition. No fully adequate study has yet been made of Wolfe's symbolism, although it has been widely recognized that he rose above the level of realistic fiction to that of imaginative symbolism.

In "The Child by Tiger" Wolfe has made abundant use of symbolism, as is indicated by the title itself. The unfolding of the story becomes an allegory of the Negro in America, the relationships between the white and black races, and Dick Prosser emerges as a symbol of the Negro race, and—in a larger sense—of the dark side of mankind's own soul. Thus, in the final analysis, he becomes a complicated symbol of the power of primeval passion.

Dick Prosser is first presented as the faithful family servant. As such he exemplifies the virtues that have made the Negro domestic in the South legendary and have brought the Southern whites to think of him as "almost a member of the family." If Dick had continued as he began, in his old age he would have been called "Uncle" Dick as a title of respect and genuine affection. His brief period of service represents the long and faithful service rendered by the Negro to the white man—the inferior to the superior race, according to Wolfe's view.

Dick's origins are wrapped in mystery. Except for the fact that he had served in the "ahmy" nothing is known about him. Wolfe says simply that "He came from darkness." Though rumors, speculations, and discussions were rife, no one ever penetrated the mystery of his past. His race likewise came out of darkness, the dark heart of the dark continent, the vast unknown and—to the white man—the unknowable. After three centuries of life in America the Negro is still a stranger to his white neighbors. The veil of mystery that surrounds his soul has not yet been penetrated.

Though far removed from the jungle in time and space, Dick bore its mark upon him. (Wolfe evidently intended this to be implied in the title when he originally called the story "The Congo.") He possessed the stealth and cunning of an animal—an animal of the jungle that could appear and disappear almost at will, an animal of prey that was seen crouching ready to spring but did not, and would merely slink away. Hence the allusion is made to the tiger as the symbol of stealth, cunning, and ferocious power when aroused, dangerous to both friend and foe—to kin and prey alike.

In striking contrast to the animal side of his nature, Dick also illustrates the Negro's natural propensity for religion and his willingness to adopt the religion of his conquerors and to fuse it into his own. Dick worshipped the white man's God, read the white man's Bible, and sang the white man's hymns, but his religion was still strangely his own: "Sometimes on these occasions his speech would be made up of some weird jargon of Biblical phrases and quotations and allusions, of which he seemed to have hundreds, and which he wove together in the strange pattern of his emotion in a sequence that was meaningless to them but to which he himself had the coherent clue." Sometimes he talked of Armageddon and the coming day of judgment and justice.

Like his race, Dick was the innocent sufferer at the hands of the white man. After Lon Pilcher drove into the car Dick was driving and struck Dick viciously in the face, not once but twice, Dick took this painful indignity without flinching, with the same stoic calm with which his race accepted the innumerable indignities heaped upon it by the white man for generations, although his hands twitched and his eyes became red like an animal's. But when his long pent-up feelings broke loose, they erupted like a volcano. His wild sweep through Libya Hill was like a maddened animal's prowl through the jungle clawing at every other animal in reach. Like an avenging angel of doom he precipitated his own personal Armageddon and swept through the town dealing out vengeance and death on every hand. Animal passion reinforced by religious might, jungle fury enhanced by the deadly weapon of civilization made Dick the terror he became—a black terror that loomed even blacker against the whiteness of falling snow. His own race was not immune, but it was the white man who suffered most.

How does Wolfe interpret this enigmatic symbol that he has created? He makes no attempt to resolve the conflicting forces; he simply recognizes them and sees in Dick Prosser the embodiment of the perpetually conflicting forces of good and evil. To Wolfe the Negro was an abiding paradox, capable of the finest qualities of humanity, "a friend, a brother," but equally representative of the worst, "a mortal enemy, an unknown demon." In the Negro two opposing worlds join, for he is both "a tiger and a child."

"The Child by Tiger" is in a sense a prophecy of "the long, hot summers" that were to come and is an explanation, if not a justification, of them. In this story Wolfe shows considerable insight into certain aspects of Negro motivation despite, rather than because of, his Southern heritage. While his Southern-ness is still clearly visible, he had undergone growth and had achieved a greater breadth and depth of vision as his humanitarian concern came to the fore.

3 The Jew:

'The Fires of Love and Hate'

No aspect of Thomas Wolfe has been more controversial, except the question of form, than his writing about the Jew. His work frequently evokes strong emotional responses in his readers, and he has been vigorously denounced as anti-Semitic and just as stoutly defended. The positions of both groups of critics are tenable, however, because of Wolfe's amazing ambivalence toward the Jew and the presence of his fiction of what Leo Gurko has called a "perpetual alternation of hate and love." [1] Wolfe's Jewish characters reflect both these extremes. While they vary in importance in his work, ranging from thumbnail sketch in the passing parade to major character in his entire tetralogy, they do fall quite naturally into five categories: student, businessman, elite society, lover, and symbol.

Three Jewish Students

A portrayal of the Jew as student would certainly be expected of an autobiographical author who spent twenty-three of his thirty-eight years in school—seventeen as student and six as teacher. Wolfe does indeed present the Jew as student and does so from three distinct points of view: as fellow student, as teacher, and as neutral observer. All three of these characters occur in the Gant cycle.

The Jew as seen through the eyes of a fellow student is Edward

Michalove, the principal Jewish character in *Look Homeward, Angel* and a student in the Altamont Fitting School. The son of a jeweler, Edward is twelve years old and has a non-Jewish appearance. The boy's life at the school was desperately unhappy and tormented for he was the object of ridicule from teachers and students alike.

Wolfe does not say whether there were other Jewish students or not; there may have been, though they would have been few in relation to the total student body. Edward is singled out as the victim of gross maltreatment and the object of hatred. At first glance this abuse appears to be just another example of the juvenile anti-Semitism which countless Jewish students in schools over the world have experienced, but though that may have entered somewhat into the total picture, the main reason that Edward was persecuted was not his Jewish blood. The quality which set him apart is not his Jewishness but his effeminacy, and it is this trait that brings down upon him the cruel persecution and hatred of his fellow students.

Wolfe does not picture the boys of Altamont as free from anti-Jewish feeling; on the contrary, he gives ample evidence of it, but shows that their attitude, although reprehensible, is less than hatred. In the years before Eugene entered the Altamont Fitting School he and his playmates considered those different from themselves as "barbarians": "Eugene, Max, and Harry ruled their little neighborhood: they made war upon the negroes and Jews, who amused them, and upon the Pigtail Alley people [poor whites of the Tobacco Road type], whom they hated and despised." Wolfe says of this mischievous trio: "They spat joyously upon the Jews," and gives as their sentiments, "Drown a Jew and hit a nigger." These boys took delight in ridiculing Jews and chased Jewish children over the neighborhood, but their activities are mild compared to the "shagging" of Jews by the Lonigan gang on Chicago's South Side.

The leader in these boyish pranks was Max Isaacs. From Max's name it might be inferred that he is Jewish, even though Wolfe informs the reader that "Harry Tarkinton and Max Isaacs were Baptists." Bearing such a Jewish sounding name may well have been the spur that made these "pogroms" a fetish with Max, just as Thomas Wolfe later reacted so strongly to any suggestions that he himself might have Jewish blood; a violent reaction constitutes a more vigorous denial of *Blutsverwandschaft*.

Actually, the general attitude toward Jews in Asheville during Wolfe's boyhood was benign. The city had a well-established and respected Jewish community, and the first state-chartered Y.M.H.A. in the entire South was established in Asheville in 1909. And it is worthy of note that Buncombe County's favorite native son, Zebulon B. Vance, was one of the nineteenth century's great champions of the Jews. Vance, North Carolina's Civil War Governor and later United States Senator, had a life-long friendship for the Jewish people and his notable address in their defense, which was widely circulated under the title *The Scattered Nation*, raised the prestige of the Jewish people throughout the South.[2] Vance's enormous popularity and influence, especially in his home region, must have aided the tolerant attitude toward the Asheville Jewish community.

After Eugene Gant's Harvard years the disappointed playwright became a reluctant teacher in the School for Utility Cultures and his experiences there are vividly recounted in *Of Time and the River*. It seemed to Eugene that he had entered a world overrun with Jews and was engulfed by them in "the brawling and ugly corridors of the university, which drowned one, body and soul, with their swarming, shrieking, shouting tides of dark amber Jewish flesh, and thence into the comparative sanctuary of the class room with its smaller horde of thirty or forty Jews and Jewesses." This situation produced the second portrait of the Jew as student, this time seen through the eyes of the teacher, and the individual singled out is the unforgettable Abraham Jones.

The extensive treatment given Abraham Jones is far greater than the attention paid to Edward Michalove and makes Jones the major Jewish character of all Wolfe's writing published during his lifetime. The brutally frank description of Abe Jones can hardly fail to arouse a strong reaction in the reader; a Jewish critic calls it "one of the most pathetic and cruel caricatures of a Jew in contemporary fiction."[3] Yet this portrayal of an intellectual Jew whom Eugene first hates and then likes is a good example—the best next to Esther Jack—of Wolfe's paradoxical attitude toward the Jew.

Abe is pictured as an eager, arrogant, and contentious student who plies Eugene with the querulous questions that every teacher knows: why didn't he assign better theme topics and use a better textbook? And in addition to being generally obnoxious, he is also consciously Jewish: why had Eugene omitted the name of Jewish writers such as Lewisohn and Sholem Asch? Thus, all the frustrations of an inexperienced and insecure teacher, fortified by an anti-Jewish prejudice, were focused on Abraham Jones, who came to be regarded as a nemesis and toward whom Eugene's dislike flamed into hatred. But eventually their differences were resolved, and the two become fast friends.

His friendship with Abe opened a new world to Eugene, one which he did not fail to exploit. When Wolfe began his teaching he was—as always—on the lookout for grist for his mill, and he hoped New York's East Side would provide fresh literary material for him during what he considered a temporary stay at New York University. He wrote Mrs. Roberts of his hope "to establish contacts here, to get material in my seven months' stay that may prove invaluable." Abe Jones proved to be that contact: "he seized upon that dreary, gray and hopeless-looking jew" and used him as an entrée to Abe's family life and history. He learned that the name Jones had been given by an "ignorant tyrant of an official" to Abe's father, an immigrant Polish Jew who spoke no English. Eugene's sense of decency is outraged at such treatment of a bewildered Jewish immigrant, but he does not take a similar view of Abe's changing his given name.

Abe's effort to disguise his racial origin behind a non-Jewish name creates strong Gentile resentment at such "deception." At first Abe tried "to rid himself of the 'accursed' Abraham" by reducing it to an initial, "A. Jones." Then he took the next step and "dared to make a final transformation, shocking, comical, pitifully clumsy in its effort at concealment and deception." Eugene discovered that the "quaint and homely 'Abe' had disappeared" and in searching the telephone directory he at length found Abe "coyly sheltered under the gentlemanly obscurity of A. Alfred Jones." This common Jewish practice of name changing is roundly condemned by Wolfe, and Abe's action is pictured as criminal. Abe "was now, in name, at any rate, a member of the great Gentile aristocracy of Jones; and just as 'Jones' had been thrust by violence upon his father, so Abe had taken violently, by theft and rape, the 'Alfred.' " Continuing in a similar but slightly more moderate vein, Wolfe heaps ridicule upon "the bravado, the effrontery, and the absurdity of the attempt" of Abe's attempted disguise and sees the effort as one foredoomed to futility: "That he should hope actually to palm himself off as a Gentile was unthinkable, because one look at him revealed instantly the whole story of his race and origin."

Wolfe's sentiments on this subject are underscored by the fact that he also treats it in *The Web and the Rock*. There, however, he softens the ridicule somewhat by placing it in the mouth of Esther Jack, who glories in her Jewish heritage, rather than making authorial comment. In the section of "Penelope's Web" where she tells George Webber that she too would like to write a book, Esther gives a list of things about which she feels deeply and would like to put into print; one of these is name changing by Jews.

> I should like to tell about Jews and Christians, and about Jews who change their names. There's this fellow Burke! Doesn't it make you want to laugh? Nathaniel Burke my eye! Why didn't he go pick a real fancy Christian name while he was about it? Montmorency Van Landingham Monteith, or Reginald Hilary Saltonstall, or Jefferson Lincoln Coolidge, or something like that? Nathaniel Burke! Can you beat it? His real name is Nathan Berkovich, I've known his people all my life.
>
> The nerve of that fellow! I get so tired of his goings on that I said to him once: "Look here, Burke. You'd just better be glad you *are* a Jew. Where would you be if it weren't for the Jews, I'd like to know. It's too bad about you."
>
> His mother and father were such nice old people. . . . They were orthodox, of course, and I think it almost killed them the way he'd acted. He won't go near them any more. Isn't it a shame —to throw that wonderful thing away in order to become an imitation Christian? [4]

This passage may have been a frank expression of Mrs. Jack's own sentiments, but they are also those of Eugene Gant prior to his reincarnation as George Webber. The example which Esther gives is reminiscent of the change made by one of Wolfe's contemporary novelists, Nathanael West, whose original name was Nathan Weinstein, though the similarity may be pure coincidence, as such cases are legion.

Wolfe's interest in names extends, of course, beyond his Jewish characters. In an unpublished sketch entitled "Margaret Proctor" he deals with the practice again. The protagonist, here called Joe Spangler, meets a woman named Margarita Restor. Spangler senses that Restor is not her "real" name and presses her for it. He learns that Restor is her married name and that her maiden name was Margaret ("Maggie") Proctor. Wolfe injects auctorial moralizing at this point.

> "What's in a name?" He had lived here in the city and observed its ways long enough to know there was a good deal. In the first place, he had noticed how often people who were most scornful over origins—who were most brilliantly cynical over the pretenses of stuff-shirted professional-Southerners, and the pontificalities of the Mayflower class, were themselves people who were living under a cloud of [squalid?] pseudonimity.

And it seemed to him to matter a good deal. For, his experience
had been, that if a man or woman had been false about his name,
the chance was great he would be false in other ways.[5]

Thus he condemns name changing as indicative of a basic falsity,
but he does so without the outraged feeling he displays when he
thinks it is an attempt to disguise racial origin. Nowhere else in
his several treatments of the subject is he as vociferous in his
denunciation of name changing as in the case of A. Alfred
Jones.

Wolfe once complained about the "Impossibility of writing a
true book about the Jew in America."[6] Since his own books
contain some of the frankest writing about the Jew in twentieth-
century literature, one may well wonder what he had in mind by
such a statement. At the time he made the observation he was just
beginning to write "O Lost," but he had already written out his
ideas about the Jew in American society.

When he left New York on his first trip to Europe in the fall of
1924, Wolfe wrote: "I had avoided having anyone come on board
to see me off; at the last moment two Jewish boys, students in my
classes of Freshman composition at New York University
appeared."[7] One of these students who came to bid the young
teacher *bon voyage* was Abe. Later when Wolfe began to write up
the account of his trip as "Passage to England" he devoted almost
all of the "2nd Installment" to his ideas about the Jew in America. He begins with a discussion of Abe as a person, then enlarges
his scope to encompass the Jewish people as a whole, and finally
ends with a consideration of Jewish religion.

> Perhaps the Jew [Abe], one day may write some words upon a
> paper—and only a word may live.
> The Jew must forget some things. He must forget to bite his
> nails when he is alone. He must forget a great deal of cant: he
> spoke to me one time of the "unbearable beauty" of something an-
> other Jew had said in a dramatic criticism. A good many Jews and
> gentiles have said it before and after. But he must forget it: it is
> cant.
> The Jew must perform a surgical operation on himself. He
> must cut his whine out. He must never, never say of himself "I am
> an artist" until he is forty; and then he must not say it until he is
> eighty—even if it should be true. And if it should be true when he
> is eighty, all the young Jews of thirty will deny it.
> The Jew must never, never talk loosely about the Philistines,
> until he knows what they are. He must never speak of "material-
> ists" scornfully until he can find a greater materialist than a poet;

he must never picture himself as a wounded stag with the hounds of the earth upon him. He must not talk too much of "beauty"; he must not decorate his room with a rusty tapestry, two Japanese prints, and a small bowl of hammered brass, because he cannot do without it. Finally, he should read Spinoza, Isaiah, and Heinrich Heine persistently.

He must learn to keep the ladies of his tribe in suspension, or he will be suspended by them—those young Rebeccas with the fine curves, and the low foreheads, and the black, hot eyes, who think too early, and too long, and too much about the same thing.

The Jew took me upon a Saturday to his room for dinner. He lived in a tenement in the East Side, noisy and encumbered with a great many small children, but otherwise not an unpleasant place. The family held the top floor: there was a straight chain of ample large rooms running from front to back. The inner rooms were dark.

His mother had prepared an excellent meal of greasy, heavy, odorous food: all the meat, he told me had been cooked the day before. He was tolerantly amused with the orthodoxy of his parents. As I remember, he said it was "the bunk."

The mother, an old woman with a friendly, sharp face, and a single wistful tooth around which swarmed a strange melange of phrases in Russian, Yiddish, with an occasional recognizable splinter of our native tongue, served the meal, but would not eat with us. His conversation with her was confined to friendly, remote monosyllables. They had, I believe, a great deal of affection ["for each other" crossed out] but they knew very little about each other. Certainly she did not know him.

Of course, the strong silent man [Calvin Coolidge] has said that no one knows a man like his mother, or at least he should have.

The Jew showed me his books after dinner. He had almost one hundred, collected patiently and cautiously at the second hand shops. He has escaped, he will escape I believe, the misery of the desire for ten thousand books. He will continue to buy a few of the good ones and suck them dry as a bone.

In addition to a volume of Pirandello's plays, and Jean Cristophe, he has recently acquired a copy of Charles Lamb's essays. He asked me if I thought he could ever imitate the manner of writing, the ease and grace and leisure and good humor of Lamb. In short, he wanted to know if he could be a gentleman. He had pictured himself, I believe, in a warm, low panelled room, before a fire reading an old book in a mellow binding, and smoking Virginia tobacco through a long pipe. There should be, perhaps, some prints on the walls of English gentleman foxhunting—what Oscar Wilde called the unspeakable in pursuit of the uneatable.

I told him that a Jew with a broad long nose would not look well in such a setting; that such an attempt would inevitably lead him to the composition of essays for the Atlantic Monthly; and that he should have to adjust his flame to a small even glow. Farther, he knew already a great deal more about a great many things than did Charles Lamb; his ideas, I thought, were better and more frequent. And his strength was in his ideas.

His ungovernable impulses, which he had described to me, to "smash things up," which came to him at times, for no apparent reason, would become a very beautiful murderous thing, most pleasant to contemplate, when he ceased firing at the landscape, and concentrated deliberately upon certain objects of his hatred. I did not think it important what they were, so long as he did not miss. The genius of his race was invective enforced by thought.

This was the Jew who came to the ship, and who may some day write some words upon a paper; and who hates many things, but who loves ideas. If what he has to say should ever reach the eyes and ears of the strong silent man, he would be pained, I am sure. He would think of a name to call the Jew. Perhaps he would call him a "radical." But, no, that would not do. We all know very well what a radical is. A radical is Senator Lafollette; Senator Borah; Senator Reed; the Reverend Fosdick; or someone who has read one of the books of the late Charles Darwin. In short, a radical is someone who declares in a firey peroration: "The time has come when I must speak my mind, whatever the consequence to my personal fortunes. Intimidated by no threats of beaureaucratic corruption, conservative stand-pattism, or reactionary hypocrisy, I declare now, once and for all, that I do not believe in Santa Claus. If this be treason, make the most of it."

This is a radical. We must find another name for the Jew. And strong, silent men do not, can not speak much. But since names for Jews come readily to the tongue of Christians, no doubt we should find one somewhere. And really we have a very responsible duty toward the Jew. We should persecute him a little more than we have recently. Indeed we have been positively unfair to him in recent years in this respect. Like the Irish, whose unquestioned predominance as an oppressed nation Bernard Shaw pointed out long ago, the Jew will [peak?] and pine if his statue as a member of a persecuted race is taken away from him.

Quite seriously, it seems that the Jew [the race] achieves his greatest triumphs under persecution: it is a mighty tonic which has enabled him to call down, through his prophets, the most splendid invective any race has ever been master of; to invoke the vengeance of his God upon his oppressors in Isaiah tones; and through his poets to blast with withering satire anyone or anything that dare oppose him. As a result he has contributed to letters and philosophy a body of literature which is, I believe, in its range, power, beauty, and importance quite unexampled. He is particularly splendid when he becomes God-intoxicated; at such a time he seems to acquire a peculiar sense of ownership in the deity, and whatever he does therefore is [couched?] with this conviction of divine preference.

It is quite impossible, however, to examine justly and intelligently the relation of the Jew to American life. Unless the analysis be eminently flattering, unless it tells a great deal about his "contributions" to the enlargement of the American society, unless a great many important and mutually unpleasant things are glossed, the long wail—that quivering Banshee cry of centuries—of persecution is raised again.

But what we do so seldom realize is that the simple fact of persecution is stupid and meaningless; the simple fact of prejudice and bigotry and intolerance is stupid and uninteresting; murder itself is a most unedifying spectacle unless we can apprehend the interior urgency that completes the act. It is a curious and disquieting reflection that the people who are forever indicating the unreasonable blindness of the passions are themselves generally incapable of discovering reasons for the blindness. They content themselves with saying: "How unreasonable! How bigoted! How cruel! Don't you know that all this is contrary to the principles of our forefathers, who most expressly abolished intolerance in the constitution; and expressed themselves in favor of a great deal of liberty and happiness for everyone? Your conduct is therefore illegal and unpatriotic."

During the course of the past two or three years I have read several hundred newspaper editorials pertaining to the organization which bears the perplexing but unusual title of Ku Klux Klan. I can remember not one of these editorials which gave a reasonable explanation for the existence of the organization—and never forget that even an unreasonable existence demands a reasonable explanation. An enormous majority of the comment has contented itself with branding the members as liars, traitors, murderers, the leaders as perjurers and swindlers, and the society itself as hostile to the safety of native institutions—accusations which may be positively true, but which do little to explain the existence of the crime.

There has been a renaissance of the ancient nonsense of "laughing it out of existence." I have never known anything to be laughed out of existence which was not first bitten by its own ridicule—the legend of Don Quixote and its demolishing effect upon the institution of chivalry is an ancient myth, no less. Funeral arrangements had already been made for knighthood when the book appeared.

It may be that some native Cervantes—perhaps Mr. Mencken of the American Mercury, who swings a heavier and a more damaging mace than the others—might smash in a similar, opened door; but our efforts at mirth in spite of our brilliant opinion of our humor, too often seems a bit savagely forced, like that of the Italian gentleman who, grinding his teeth, yells in strangled voice: "You think I am mad! But no—eet ees ver' fon-ee. I laugh—like thees—Ha! Ha! Ha!"

With the Jew, again, the business is much more complicated. We have undoubtedly a growing commercial jealousy of him, which has aroused in the small towns, as well as in the cities, the greatest bitterness. But we have no right to complain of the Jew's commercial success. If he has succeeded commercially to the discomfort of his Christian brothers, it is because they have created a commercial life whose conditions fit him like a glove. We are very young at the game of keeping an eye on the main chance, there is something very naïve in all our wisdom for ourselves: we are children who have begun to buy and sell; we are hopelessly outmatched at the beginning in any such rivalry with people to whom our greatest subtleties of trade seem banal; who have inherited all the shrewdness of five thousand years of trading; and who, at the age of two, begin to finger their father's coat sleeve deftly in order to judge the quality of the cloth.

Yet this is not the sole reason for the intensity of the feeling which exists, which we know exists, and which we are very foolish to deny. The Jew has everywhere insisted in maintaining a religious and social isolation, and where he has discarded the religious isolation, he has held to the social. This is his right, but every nation is an island and one may live upon an island, but one may not, without complication, create an island upon an island. He demands a walled city for himself, in which he may live, without ingression, and from which he may go to share in Every suffrage of the nation. Wherever he has been, wherever he goes, he has been confronted with the problem of God and the law. He entreats the right to other people's law, but he insists on his own right to furnish his own God; and two Gods and one Caesar is a difficult, an almost insoluble combination.

[Unnumbered page inserted here]

It is not that we have made of our God a God of battles—there was eternal wisdom there—but that we have made of him a God of victories, that I complain. Monotonous and pre-assured victory —ah, how destructive a thing to devotion, to leadership that is. Men are cloven to fealty by defeat far more than by triumph. It is not Austerlitz that counts; it is Waterloo.

With what mad perversity have we made of the scaffold a symbol of triumph; it is a symbol of defeat.

[Numbered pages continue]

It has been held by many that the remarkable evidence of the Jew's persistence is that he has maintained his race while losing his nation; but it is doubtless because of this rather than in spite of it that he exists. For it is quite often not the absence of empire which kills a people, but the possession of it. The Jew unharmed by civil strife, political dissension, and the ambitions for Empire of rapacious and uncompassionate rulers, save when these evils have been imposed on him by alien hands, has had, it seems to me, unequalled opportunity for survival.

Perhaps, after all, the benedictions of his particular god have fallen over him; perhaps, after all in some subtly ironic manner which we do not discern, he has been actually chosen for survival by release from all the decimating effects of nationalism.

He has been eternally right in making of his god a god of battles, but why has he, so often the defeated and the bound, made of his god a god of victories as well, and why have we, who have followed him so largely in his conceptions, made of our god the eternal victor, when our own worlds have crumbled and broken before us?

This is a strange mad paradox, it is perverse, too, for it comes from no genuine need within us. Omnipotence is not a necessary attribute of the deity. The defeated are loyal to the defeated, not to the victorious. Men do not remember Austerlitz, but Waterloo. We are mad, mad, to think of a defeated army under the leadership of a triumphant general. It can not be!

Perhaps God, too, will one day learn the mighty stratagem of defeat. What strength will then be His! [8]

Thus it was his student, the faithful Abe, who caused Wolfe to crystallize his views on the Jew and to write down these impressions as they were held by him at age twenty-four. The importance of the above passage, therefore, rests not only in the additional assessment of the character of Abe but also in giving an uninhibited account of Wolfe's attitude toward and understanding of the Jew prior to his meeting Aline Bernstein.

In the autumn of 1926 (while he was writing *Look Homeward, Angel*) Wolfe spent almost six weeks at Oxford. During this visit, which was financed by Mrs. Bernstein, he stayed at Hilltop Farm on the outskirts of the town but spent considerable time at the university. An Asheville friend, William J. Cocke, was a Rhodes scholar at Merton College, and through him Wolfe met a number of others. Wolfe duly recounts his impressions of the Rhodes scholars in *Of Time and the River* and therein gives his third portrait of the Jew as student, for one of the Rhodes scholars was "a Jew named Fried."

This time Eugene views the Jewish student from the standpoint of a neutral observer. Fried's position is, in some respects, an

enviable one; he holds one of the most coveted of scholarships and
is in his third year at the English-speaking world's most presti-
gious university, but as a Jew—and a city one at that—he is still
an outsider, even to the little group of Americans, and his lot is
not a happy one. In fact, the picture that Wolfe paints of the
group of Rhodes men is very dismal. They are frustrated and
bewildered by the hostile aloofness of Oxford, the result of which
was to produce in all except Johnny Park and Fried a sense of
utter defeat.

Fried's success in maintaining his own integrity did not win
friendly admiration from the other Rhodes scholars. He is not an
attractive person, and has what Wolfe describes as "the aggressive,
abusive, curiously uprighteous quality of his race." The others are
united in their attitude toward Fried, none of them liked him, but
they have "a strange, secret, and unwilling respect for him."

Wolfe has a respect for Fried, too, even though it may be an
unwilling one, and he recognizes that this respect is rooted, curiously, in the very reason for his original dislike of Abraham
Jones—Fried is a city Jew. His very triumph results from his
origin. As a Jew he is one of a people who have been since Biblical
times in an alien and hostile environment and who have ever
struggled against tremendous odds to maintain their identity.
Unlike some of the other scholars, Fried could not claim England
as his ancestral home, yet he was told, as they were, that as an
English speaker he was returning to the "old home." Fried jeered
at this idea: "Christ! It never was a home to me! I'd have felt
more at home if they had sent me to Siberia!" and the plaintive
truth of Jewish history sounds through the jeer. Not only was he a
Jew but a city Jew, for Fried unmistakably bore the stamp of the
city. Eugene realized that all he had seen and learned of the city
was here concentrated in one man with "a character that was
hard, bitter, unforgettably itself, and that no change of sky or
land or custom, nor the huge impact of all the alien and formida-
ble pageantry of the earth, could ever alter by a jot." Thus it is
the rock-hard character of the American city Jew that enabled
Fried, in the Faulknerian phrase, not only to endure but to
prevail.

Wolfe could admire "open courage" and "unashamed conviction." His own struggles to maintain his identity in alien and
hostile New York were much too fresh for him not to be an avid
witness of this Oxford drama. He was also passionately patriotic,
and Fried's genuine affection for America was not lost on him.
Although Fried is bound by blood to Edward Michalove and

Abraham Jones, the portrait of the Jewish student at ancient
Oxford has a ring of grudging admiration in it that is lacking in
those of the weak and effeminate student at the Altamont Fitting
School and of the pathetic and loyal student at the School for
Utility Cultures, and demonstrates far better than they do the
ability of the Jew to persevere and to survive.

The Jew as Businessman

Instances of Jewish businessmen are naturally more numerous
than those of Jewish students in Wolfe's writing. His Jewish
businessmen (and businesswomen) are, however, of two economic
levels: those of the Gant cycle and the Libya Hill period of the
Webber cycle, few though they be, are small business people but
those of the later Webber cycle—after he has met Esther Jack—
are wealthy representatives of big business. Hence his portraits of
the Jew as businessman encompass a wide economic range.

Jewish businessmen are most conspicious in *Look Homeward,
Angel* by their almost complete absence. Except for the old grocer
with dirty hands and the pawnbroker with shady ethics, none of
Altamont's Jewish businessmen appears in *Look Homeward,
Angel.* Nor is *Of Time and the River* much more populated with
Jewish businessmen than its predecessor, for here there are only
three. Samuel Friedman, the Boston realtor, is altogether lacking
in the qualities Eugene admires in the Jewish people, a condition
that Wolfe half-humorously attributes to the Boston climate. The
other two are Abe Jones's brother and sister, both of whom exhibit a pertinacious toughness that results in business success.

Abe's older brothers had a zinc business in the "gas-house district" of the East Side, and a brief glimpse of one of them, Barney,
is given. The difficulties of a poor Jew, a first-generation American, conducting a business in one of the toughest areas of the city
are numerous, not the least of which is gangsterism. Gangsters
came to Barney's shop regularly demanding money, which the
merchants of the district paid "meekly and regularly for
'protection.'" But Barney refused and, although his shop had
been frequently robbed, he fought the gangsters with tooth and
claw. Preparation for business on such a brutal level had been
afforded Barney in youthful combat on the city streets, and his
survival under such conditions is a success in itself and arouses
Eugene's sympathy and admiration.

Abe's sister, Sylvia, receives much more extended portraiture than Barney, though Wolfe is far more interested in other aspects of Sylvia's life than her business activities. She is to him the very personification of the "highly enamelled city woman." Like the rest of her family Sylvia had been thrown on her own resources since childhood, yet her disappointments in life, such as her unhappy romance that left her with an illegitimate son, had not impeded her drive to business success. Beginning as a salesgirl she then worked in a millinery shop and finally had her own "hat shop" on Second Avenue where she did a thriving business and employed several assistants. Sylvia represents the penniless immigrant woman who by her own shrewdness and terrific drive achieved a considerable success in business. She is generous to her family, but she displays the unmistakable mark of triumph over earlier impecunity, "a fortune in jewelry blazed heavily and shockingly on her bony little hands."

The picture of the Jew as businessman during Eugene-George's Asheville, Boston, and early New York years is thus one of small merchants. The liaison of George Webber and Esther Jack, however, brought other types of Jewish businessmen into his ken, and two of these occur in *The Web and the Rock;* Mr. Rosen the wealthy merchant and Mr. Rawng the prosperous publisher—one of Wolfe's most favorable and one of his most baleful Jewish portraits.

Mr. Rosen's position in the business world had been won with difficulty; he was a self-made man who sprang from "plodding Jews of the middle class." Beginning with a small shop on the East Side, the firm of Stein and Rosenberg had moved a long way uptown and was now located on fashionable Fifth Avenue. In the course of this prosperous migration the firm had lost its name; Mr. Rosenberg was now Mr. Rosen. This name changing, usually an occasion for caustic comment by Wolfe, is not at all censured because Mr. Rosen "had changed his name, but he made no effort to change his race or his identity." Mr. Rosen, to the contrary, gloried in the fact that he was Jewish.

In some respects the portrait of Mr. Rosen is that of a conventional wealthy merchant.[9] He takes his family to France on his buying trips and establishes them at Deauville. He enjoys the luxury of a private deck on the great transatlantic liners, sends his son to Oxford, and otherwise enjoys the accouterments of wealth. But he departs from the tradition of merchant prince in one important particular, which Wolfe considered distinctive—he lived over his shop.

Further, Mr. Rosen had always lived over his shop. He began it
in two rooms on Grand Street, and he continued it now in two
floors and eighteen rooms on Fifth Avenue. And he will continue
it, also, in the new and more splendid building now being erected
farther uptown. There he will have the top three floors, twenty-
four rooms, and the best view in town. When a Christian makes
money out of his shop, or another man's shop, he moves out as
soon as he can. He goes up the Hudson, buys a thousand acres and
forty rooms, and gets gardeners and hostlers from England. Not so
Mr. Rosen. His ideas went back to the Fuggers, the Cabots, the
early Rothchilds. He lived over his shop and had lots of the very
best champagne for dinner.[10]

Wolfe obviously approves of Mr. Rosen and especially of his
manner of living. Not only is the language in Mr. Rosen's portrait
favorable but the tone is also sympathetic. The self-made man
appealed to Wolfe more than one who had inherited wealth, but
above this was a quality which Wolfe greatly admired and one
which he associated with the Jew—the innate ability not just to
gain wealth but rather to derive genuine pleasure from wealth. It
is in discussing this quality, which forms the foundation of his
great respect for Mr. Rosen, that Wolfe gives one of his ringing
tributes to the Jews which is so out of harmony with his accusations against them, but nonetheless is genuinely sincere.

> . . . Mr. Rosen had a very princely quality—the princely quality
> that almost all rich Jews have, and that few rich Christians ever
> get. Wealth is difficult to attain, but it is good, pleasant, desirable
> —therefore let those with wealth enjoy it.
> There is, of course, no greater fallacy than the one about the
> stinginess of Jews. They are the most lavish and opulent race on
> earth.[11]

Wolfe's tendency to make sweeping generalizations accounts for
this statement in which he reverses the complaint of Mr. Riah, the
noble and generous Jew in Dickens' *Our Mutual Friend*, who
observes:

> Men find the bad among us easily enough—among what peo-
> ples are the bad not easily found?—but they take the worst of us as
> samples of the best; they take the lowest of us as presentations of
> the highest; and they say, "All Jews are alike." [12]

Just as Wolfe has sometimes taken the worst examples and made
them universal, so he takes one of what he considers the best and
makes it universal. In his broad generalizations he is consistent
only in saying that all Jews are alike.

There is also the possibility that another factor entered into the portrait of Mr. Rosen which makes an analogy with Mr. Riah appropriate. In the characterization of Mr. Riah, Dickens is attempting to make amends for Fagin and to answer some of the criticism he had received. It is likely that Wolfe in portraying Mr. Rosen is also trying to answer some of the criticism he received after the publication of *Of Time and the River* and perhaps make amends for Abraham Jones and Fried.

Edith Linder, Esther's sister, is portrayed as an immensely able woman who has played a large part in the achievement of Stein and Rosen's. But she remains a background figure, shy and silent. Although she is overshadowed by the ebullient Esther, Edith has great success in the highly competitive world of New York fashions. As a businesswoman she is an upper class counterpart of Sylvia Jones.

One of Wolfe's most caustic satires is his account of the publishing firm of Rawng and Wright, which he entitled "The Philanthropists," and the bulk of his attack is directed at the senior partner, Mr. Hyman Rawng. In the first place, Mr. Rawng, who had been born Rawngstein, is guilty of changing his name, and this is greeted with the sneering comment, "in the interests of brevity, no doubt." Mr. Rawng is Oriental-looking and has a thick accent, boorish mannerisms, and an utter lack of any semblance of business ethics. His method of dealing with young authors is to take them to a speakeasy, fill them with liquor, overwhelm them with hypocritical lying, and then take every economic advantage of them possible. Mr. Rawng's partner, Mr. Wright, is not given much notice in this portrayal, but he is of the same stripe as Rawng. Wolfe culminates this satire by a rare resort to verse in the spirit of the oft-parodied "Trees."

The provocation of this satire is plain: Rawng and Wright rejected George Webber's book. Esther Jack had given them the manuscript because she knew Wright. Though Rawng turned the manuscript down, it was Wright who "five weeks later" wrote George the letter of rejection.

> While the writing shows an occasional trace of talent, it seems to us that the work as a whole is without sufficient merit to justify its publication, and moreover, of such enormous length that even if a publisher were found who was willing to print it, it would be extremely difficult to find readers who would be willing to read it. . . . The book is obviously autobiographical, and since we published at least a half dozen books just like this last year, and lost money on all of them, we don't see how we could risk money on

your book, particularly since the writing is so unskillful, amateurish, and repetitive as practically to annihilate what small chances of success such a book might have.[13]

The sting of rejection thus accounts for a satire in whose tone a personal authorial pique is clearly audible. The resulting picture of the Jew as publisher is written with a pen dipped in acid. Although Wolfe implies Rawng is Jewish, he does not identify him as such—unlike most occasions where he quickly pins a label on his Jewish characters—until Webber later retrieves the manuscript and informs Esther about it. In reply to her question to whom he talked, George simply says, "A Jew."

The close parallel which Wolfe maintains between the account of George Webber's *Home to Our Mountains* and the pre-publication history of *Look Homeward, Angel* makes the identity of the firm which served as unwitting model for Rawng and Wright quite clear. Elizabeth Nowell recounts the initial efforts to find a publisher for Wolfe's manuscript which he completed in the spring of 1928.

> Mrs. Bernstein first took the manuscript to Boni & Liveright, but after five weeks' consideration, their editor declined it saying: "It is so long—so terribly long—that it is most difficult for a reader to sustain an interest to the end. One cannot deny that much of it has quality, if not originality—on the whole it is a pattern—the autobiography of a young man—and so much of it has been done, and so often, that we hesitate to take another chance . . ." Wolfe went into one of his fits of deep depression.[14]

The firm of Boni and Liveright was but eleven years old when the manuscript of *Look Homeward, Angel* was submitted to it. The manuscript was read by two readers, Louis Kronenberger and Beatrice Kaufman, and the rejection letter was written by editor T. R. Smith. Boni and Liveright was not the only publisher to reject *Look Homeward, Angel,* but it was the first, and the fact that it was Jewish-owned did nothing to salve the wounded pride of the young author. Both Wolfe's adolescent sensitiveness and anti-Jewish prejudice are evident in the portrayal of Mr. Rawng.

Wolfe uses the name "Rawng and Wright" to be in keeping with the dual name of the firm, a standard practice in his fictional nomenclature. While he apparently had T. R. Smith in mind in the characterization of Wright, since he parodies Smith's letter and attributes it to Wright, he makes the main target of this satire the flamboyant Horace Liveright.

The publishing house presided over by Liveright during the Roaring Twenties was an aggregation of talent whose unorthodox methods and behavior can perhaps best be described by the word "zany"; in fact, the Boni and Liveright office has been described by one who worked there as "the Jazz Age in microcosm." The wild parties both during and after office hours are legendary; liquor flowed not only around the offices but through them. T. R. Smith's "stingers" are celebrated, and Arthur Pell (the office manager) complained about Liveright's bills from bootleggers. Wolfe's accusation of "publishing by intuition" was not unfounded, for Liveright played his "hunches" to the limit. Yet the achievements of the firm are notable. One of its most famous innovations was the origination of the Modern Library—now published by Bennett Cerf, a onetime Liveright employee. Liveright was the first publisher to become actively interested in Eugene O'Neill; he published *An American Tragedy,* which brought Dreiser his long-overdue recognition, and Van Loon's *Story of Mankind* after it had been rejected by seventeen other publishers; he helped to advance the fortunes of Faulkner and Hemingway, among many others. Actually Liveright had few dictums about publishing, but one of them was "his rule about young authors that their first books should always receive a chance, on the theory that the second book might be good." [15] No wonder Wolfe was doubly disappointed for his book to be rejected by the publisher who was supposed to give an unknown his fairest hearing. But the Liveright magic failed to spot the potentiality of *Look Homeward, Angel* and not only missed the chance which Scribner's took, but also became the prototype for Wolfe's caustic though comic satire.

The Jew as stockbroker is shown in the person of Esther's husband, Frederick Jack, in *You Can't Go Home Again,* where his portrait is favorably and studiously drawn. In his delineation of Mr. Jack, Wolfe employs one of his favorite ideas about character analysis: you can best tell what a person is like by watching him get up in the morning and prepare for the day's work. (He also applied the same technique to Esther Jack, Foxhall Edwards, and James Wyman, Sr.—the banker in "The Lion at Morning.") The resulting portrait of Mr. Jack is the conventional wealthy broker whose name is too obvious a symbol even to bear comment.

Mr. Jack resides on Park Avenue and thoroughly enjoys the luxuries his wealth has brought him. The depiction of his opulence also shows Wolfe's love for specific detail: Mr. Jack's slippers

are "red Russian leather," his shaving brush is a "large silver-han-
dled" one, his underwear is "of the finest silk, and he had more
than forty suits from London." There is about Mr. Jack's whole
life a Germanic love of order which he maintains with dignity,
and he permits no unseemly intrusion from the feverish world of
speculation in which he worked. His wealth and sense of security
permit him to take a benevolent view of what was wasted or stolen
by his corps of retainers. Like his fellows "he gambled every day
upon the price of stocks" but without fear for "the empire of
American business . . . was his faith, his fortune, and his life."
Wolfe concludes that "In all these ways Mr. Frederick Jack was
not essentially different from ten thousand other men of his class
and position."

One of the distinguishing features of Mr. Jack's portrait is that
its tone is one of cool restraint. Even the Jewish label is attached
to him with a delicacy that for Wolfe is unusual. Mr. Jack likes to
have "the better sort of actors, artists, writers, and wealthy, cultivated Jews around his table." His pleasures come each in its
proper time and place, but he does not overindulge because "His
ancient and Hebraic spirit was tempered with a classic sense of
moderation." His balanced understanding is attributed by Wolfe
to "some great inheritance of suffering, the long, dark ordeal of
his race." Such oblique references are far removed from the im-
passioned accusations George Webber hurls at Esther. But the
portrait of Mr. Jack is not drawn in anger; it is painted with a
studied objectivity and a feeling of respect.

After Aline Bernstein published *Three Blue Suits* in 1933,
Wolfe wrote her a congratulatory letter in which he comments: "I
don't know if Herbert Wilson has an actual counterpart in life as
has Mr. Froelich or Eugene." The character Eugene Lyons is of
course Wolfe himself, and Wolfe takes that of Mr. Froelich to be
based on Mrs. Bernstein's husband. After discussing his own activities for some length Wolfe proceeds to take Mrs. Bernstein to task
for her portrayal of himself and her husband.

> I don't believe that you really think of your husband and me as
> you have portrayed us in these stories. I am sorry that you said
> some of the things you did, and that you have been willing to give
> out to the world these portraits as representing your own estimates
> of us. Perhaps it is false for the artist to picture people as being
> better than they are, but I think it even more false to picture them
> as being worse, and I do think that in your stories about Mr. Froe-
> lich and Eugene, you have sometimes been uncharitable and un-
> just, and that you could have shown them as better people than

you make them, without injuring the truth or quality of your writing.

Wolfe, who has done this very thing to scores of people, now finds himself in the uncomfortable position of serving as model, and the shoe on his own foot pinches. However, in the very next paragraph of the letter he goes on to defend Mrs. Bernstein's husband.

> I never got to know your husband very well and I don't suppose there was much love lost between us, but you did tell me many times that he had many fine and generous qualities—a generous devotion to his family and children and great liberality and affection for friends of the family and some of your own friends who were down on their luck, which he demonstrated time and time and again by helping them. Don't you think since this is true, you could have made this element in his character plain without injuring your story? You made him a leathery-hearted broker with hardly a spark of generous affection left in him, and I think you are unfair in doing this.[16]

Mrs. Bernstein vehemently denied that Mr. Froelich in any way resembled her husband. Whether Wolfe had this exchange of views in mind when he portrayed Frederick Jack is of course uncertain, but Jack is depicted as "kind and temperate"; throughout he is generous and tolerant and his solicitious consideration for his family and friends is shown in numerous instances, such as in the scenes after the fire has interrupted Esther's party. One cannot definitely assert that Wolfe's Frederick Jack is intended as a corrective portrayal of Mr. Froelich, but such an assumption is well within the limits of possibility. If it is so intended, then the role of Wolfe as defender of Esther's husband is indeed an ironical one.

Whatever else may be said of him, Theodore Bernstein was a broker and an affluent man. He was born in Bad Ems, Germany, came to the United States at sixteen, and had a long business career in New York. Prior to 1932 he was associated with the brokerage firm of Bache and Company, one of Wall Street's biggest. In that year he was one of the founders of Carl M. Loeb, Rhoades and Company and was a partner in this brokerage house until his death in 1957 at the age of eighty-four. At the time of his death he resided at 875 Park Avenue.

Wolfe did not rely entirely on Mrs. Bernstein for information about her husband. His notebook for the first half of 1931 contains much research material on Theodore Bernstein drawn from

New York City directories, newspaper files, and other sources. But in many instances Wolfe did use anecdotes which may have come from Mrs. Bernstein or, possibly, Bernstein himself.

In unpublished portions of the Jack story Wolfe gives an account of Jack's (Jacobs in the manuscript) boyhood in Germany. The section with the typed title of "Morning" (the subtitle, "The Dream," is in Aswell's handwriting) shows young Frederick in a class in Koblenz, where the teacher asks him the Latin word for farmer. Dreaming about America, he cannot think of *agricola* and only mumbles "ag—ag." Later he is taunted by two of his classmates in a scene in which Wolfe takes pains to show Germanic anti-Semitism long before the era of Adolph Hitler.

> "No. He'll never know the word for farmer," Walter Grauschmidt answered calmly and with assurance. "He'll know the word for money. He'll know the word for cash. He'll know the word for interest and loan in every language in the world. But he'll never know the word for farmer."
>
> "Why?" said Albert Hartmann looking at his more gifted and intellectual companion with a stupid stare.
>
> "Why," said Walter Grauschmidt deliberately, "because he is a Jew, that's why. A farmer has to work hard with his hands. And there never was a Jew who would work hard with his hands if he could help it. He lets the others do that sort of work, while he sits back and takes the money in. They are a race of pawnbrokers and money lenders. My father told me." He turned to Frederick and spoke quietly and insultingly to him. "That's right, isn't it? You don't deny it, do you?" [17]

In another passage, entitled "Morning: Jack Asleep," Jacobs (Jack) dreams he is back in his childhood home in Germany and his family still treats him as a child rather than as the successful American businessman he has become. He attends a reunion of his classmates, including the two who taunted him in the above passage. Though he intended to gloat and brag about his success in America, he cannot bring himself to do so.[18]

Nothing in the unpublished parts of the Jack story substantially alters the published portrait of Frederick Jack. In an unpublished fragment called "The Madman" Wolfe pictures Jack's senior partner, Rosenthal, as a brilliant but unbalanced broker who is going crazy, though no one seems to be aware of his deteriorating condition except his secretary, Miss Feinberg.[19] The inclusion of Rosenthal's portrait, which Aswell deleted, would only have enhanced that of Jack. In contrast to Rosenthal's erratic behavior

Jack looms even larger as a stable, respectable broker who remains singularly aloof from the feverish world of speculation.

In his presentation of Jewish businessmen Wolfe attributes unethical practices to only two: Saul Stein, the Altamont pawnbroker, and Hyman Rawng. He does, in fact, seem to have purposely avoided evoking the hoary stereotype of the sharp and unethical Jewish trader. In the one case where he overtly discusses business ethics *per se* he excuses the offender and gives a long explanation for his behavior. In the unpublished "Ike Brown" he takes the career of Abe Jones further than he does anywhere in his published work. Abe's brother died and Abe took over the operation of his business. After describing various changes which took place in Abe as the result of his business career, Wolfe ponders the reasons.

> How then could such a man be capable of this revolting trickery and cunning? The answer was simple: although highly scrupulous in his personal and friendly relations with people, Abe [*sic*] had been brought up in the belief that business was a kind of cutthroat duel to the death, in which any weapon was allowable, and any means of securing victory, a good one, if it worked. . . .
>
> Finally, Abe now regarded himself as the responsible head of his family: like most Jews, his sense of family loyalty was very strong, his first, almost entire duty was to them, and he thought he was justified in using any means that would preserve to them intact from any aggression the estate and the business his brother had accumulated.[20]

Though Wolfe deplores Abe's business ethics, he finds justification for them in Abe's urban background, strong sense of family loyalty, and early poverty. Wolfe leaves no doubt that he intends Abe Jones and Frederick Jack to represent opposite economic extremes. In his notebook he once wrote:

> A family of poor New York Jews (Abes family)
> A family of rich New York Jews (Alines family) [21]

The differences between these two groups are not only social, cultural, and economic, but according to Wolfe's fictional portrayal they extend even to business ethics.

The portraits of the Jew as businessman in the later Webber cycle are dominated by wealth and affluence. With the exception of Hyman Rawng's they are more objectively and sympathetically drawn than the earlier and briefer ones in the Gant and early Webber cycles.

Members of an Elite Society

The social world into which Esther Jack sought to introduce George Webber was not quite that of the Social Registerites but it was an elite society. The Jew as a member of this elite society is revealed by the guests at Mrs. Jack's party. Wolfe places the date of this party as October 17, 1929, just prior to the stock market crash, to dramatize the weaknesses in America immediately preceding that catastrophic event. Though Mrs. Jack's circle of friends is both wide and heterogeneous and her guests come from a variety of backgrounds, the majority of those who are named bear Jewish names. The women include an idle heiress, Lily Mandell, and a woman of achievement, Roberta Heilprinn; the men are of such varied types as the aged rake, Jake Abramson, and the urbane banker, Lawrence Hirsch. But all have at least one quality in common, they are cultured and polished.

Miss Lily Mandell is a beautiful heiress of Midas wealth whose sensual charms are incarnate in the word "voluptuous." She likes to assume a pose of superior intellectualism by displaying an interest in such an unlikely subject as Thomas Lovell Beddoes. Wolfe brands this intellectualism as spurious by a jab at one of his favorite targets among contemporary authors: "there was really no way for her to learn anything new, except, possibly, through a quiet talk with Mr. T. S. Eliot." But compared to the dissolute heiress, Amy Carlton, she becomes a more favorable representative of the idle rich.

Roberta Heilprinn, a woman of achievement, is an extremely rare portrait in the Wolfe gallery—that of an Israelite in whom there is no guile. Her ability as director of "a famous art theatre" had won her homage even from her enemies. Her appearance is handsome and striking and her face is a blandness without hypocrisy. Though she cloaks her shrewdness with suaveness, there is no hint of crafty subterfuge. Such completely favorable portraits are exceedingly scarce in Wolfe's teeming world.

Mr. Cargill sees this "completely flattering, thinly disguised portrait of Theresa Helburn as Miss Heilprinn" as evidence that Wolfe did not abandon the idea of writing for the theatre, and accuses Wolfe of ulterior motive: "Wolfe realized that Miss Helburn occupied the throne of power in the Theatre Guild and he might need her favor some day." [22] Wolfe may have still nursed hopes for *Welcome to Our City* or one of his other plays, but it had been a long time since his original fury at the Guild (1923) and despite Vardis Fisher's statement that Wolfe "never forgot what he took to be a slight or a meanness and he never forgave it," [23] furious Thomas may have mellowed. Miss Helburn was a remarkable woman, and no evidence has been presented to show that Wolfe did not genuinely admire her at that time. He was certainly elated in 1929 when Miss Helburn invited him to the dress rehearsal of the Guild's production of O'Neill's *Dynamo,* where he sat by Lynn Fontanne.

Without doubt Miss Helburn's kindnesses to Wolfe were the result of her friendship with Mrs. Bernstein, as she makes clear in her autobiography.

> The love affair between Aline and Thomas Wolfe went on for years, as all the world knows now. Tom was a great talker with a terrific flow of words. (Somewhere in one of his great sprawling novels is a page describing me. I tried to find it to insert here, but I bogged down in Tom's prose.) His bitter anti-Semitism and the ruthless way he used it to inflict pain on Aline made it most difficult for me to like him.[24]

Miss Helburn thus becomes one of the very few of Wolfe's models to admit in print that she is the prototype of one of his characters, and even she is cagey about which one she is. But she could afford to make a frank admission; most of his other models did not fare nearly so well in the transformation from reality to fictional character.

The aged rake, Jake Abramson, upon whom the mark of the fleshpots was plain, is one of Wolfe's more unpleasant portraits, not because he was old, subtle, sensual, weary, but because Wolfe invokes a grotesque image almost without parallel in his writing to brand Abramson: "he had the face of a vulture." Yet even this is slightly tempered. Jake's stroking of Esther's arm was "a gesture frankly old and sensual, jaded, and yet strangely fatherly and gentle." Abramson humorously regales Esther and Miss Heilprinn with an account of the horrors of being on a diet at Carlsbad (the Czechoslovakian spa) and the food of an English ship. The ship's food he informs them with "cynic humor in his weary eyes" was "fit for nothing but a bunch of goys!" The use of this Yiddish term of derision for Gentiles and the mirth it provoked reveals to Webber in a flash the unifying bonds of Jewry and its ancient and proud separateness from the Gentile world.

One of the most striking guests at the party is Lawrence Hirsch, the banker. His regal and courtly bearing makes him stand out even in a distinguished group. Though he is a gracious man, his features "were vested in unconscious arrogance with the huge authorities of wealth." Yet he is no grasping robber baron; rather he is allied with the liberal causes of the 1920's which the intellectuals held dear, such as the Sacco-Vanzetti case. His interest in this *cause célèbre* is not surprising as it was the one event of the decade which succeeded in arousing intellectuals of every kind. Mr. Hirsch is "the very model of what a great captain of finance, letters, arts, and enlightened principles should be," an improved modern version of Disraeli's Sidonia.

In describing Mr. Hirsch's wooing of Lily Mandell, Wolfe writes a paragraph liberally embedded with quotations and paraphrases from the Biblical Song of Solomon.

> He did not take her aside and say: "Thou art fair, my love; behold, thou art fair, thou hast doves' eyes." Nor did he say: "Tell me, O thou whom my soul loveth, where thou feedest." He did not remark to her that she was beautiful as Tirzah, or comely as Jerusalem, or terrible as an army with banners. He did not ask anyone to stay him with flagons, or comfort him with apples, or confess that he was sick of love. And as for saying to her: "Thy navel is like a round goblet, which wanteth not liquor; thy belly is like an heap of wheat set about with lilies," the idea had never occurred to him.[25]

This may seem at first glance only a sly attempt to label Mr. Hirsch a Jew by associating him with the Hebrew lover in the Canticles, but that is not Wolfe's intent. Wolfe is portraying Mr. Hirsch as a man of restraint whose thorough self-discipline permits no such display of his emotions. Actually, Wolfe is contrasting Mr. Hirsch as a lover with himself as lover (perhaps unconsciously) in his own tempestuous wooing of Esther. It was Wolfe who said of his love in the final chapter of *Of Time and the River*, "Esther was fair; she was fair; she had dove's eyes." This recurring image is taken from Song of Solomon 1:15, "Behold, thou art fair, my love; behold, thou art fair; thou hast doves' eyes." This verse from Wolfe's favorite book of the Bible next to Ecclesiastes seemed to him the perfect image for his Hebrew sweetheart. By saying that such a thought had never occurred to Mr. Hirsch, Wolfe seems to be implying not only that such a reference would be inconsistent with his character and temperament, but also that the worldly, erudite Mr. Hirsch is lacking in his knowledge of what Wolfe thinks is one of the greatest pieces of Hebrew literature. The religious heritage of the Jews never rises to the surface in any of Wolfe's Jewish characters except Abe Jones's mother.

The view of an elite society, represented by these four characters, is hardly of the Olympian level of Jewish society known as the "Jewish Grand Dukes," but it is definitely an upper, privileged group whose qualifications rest on either wealth or successful personal attainment and may include both, but above all must also include the urban polish and pretense at intellectualism that the 1920's made a cultural and social shibboleth.

A Jewish Lover

Wolfe writes of love with the same lack of reticence he shows in discussing other personal experiences. In his tetralogy along with various infatuations he records four instances when he fell in love; two of these occur in the Gant cycle, Laura James and Ann, and two in the Webber cycle, Esther Jack and Else von Kohler. But the preëminent love was not the Nordic beauty, nor the idealized Laura James, nor Ann the Bostonian, so wildly wooed in romantic Paris; the supreme love was Esther Jack, George's Jewish paramour, whose prototype was—as all the world knows—Aline Frankau Bernstein.[26] In her the Jew as lover becomes incarnate.

This famous romance, one of the most celebrated in American literature, is unique in that the reading public possesses fictional accounts of the affair by both participants. The woman's side appeared in print first. Early in the relationship Wolfe has Esther exclaim: "God, I wish I could write! If I only knew how to put it down I know I could write a wonderful book." This repeated desire of Esther's finally came to fruition when Mrs. Bernstein published her novel *The Journey Down,* and it is illuminating in a discussion of the romance to consider this work also. Nothing more clearly shows Wolfe's ambiguity toward the Jew than George Webber's romance with Esther Jack.

George Webber met Esther on board the *Vesuvia* in August 1925 while returning from his first trip to Europe. Though the actual name of the ship, *Olympic,* on which the meeting took place seemed suitable enough, Wolfe's choice of a volcano for the fictional name of the ship is even more appropriate. Following the meeting passionate love erupted with volcanic fury. But the ill-fated romance was doomed from the beginning. At the time of the meeting Mrs. Bernstein was forty-two, seventeen years older than

Wolfe, already partially deaf, married (when Wolfe was two years old) to a man with whom she lived congenially all her life, and the mother of a grown son and daughter. Yet in spite of these amazing differences there rapidly developed a romance which flamed for five years, and when it ended cost him years of bitterness and brooding and drove her to attempted suicide.[27] The nature of this *grande affaire* was described by Mrs. Bernstein almost twenty years after it ended (and twelve years after Wolfe's death) with disarming frankness.

> It was a supreme experience, the most wonderful thing in the world. The most important thing between us was our feeling for each other. It was a deep, passionate love, added to a clear fine friendship. Personal things were always coming between us, his intense jealousy of me, one thing and another. Our real companionship was beyond anything anyone can imagine, often so gay and filled with laughter. We shared a sense of beauty in poetry and painting that enriched our lives, brought everything to twice its value. This is what remains to me of Tom.[28]

Whatever else may be said of this romance, it is an irrefutable fact that the great love of Wolfe's life was Mrs. Bernstein.

In addition to those barriers between the two already mentioned there was another, and one not less great: Mrs. Bernstein was Jewish. In the description of the meeting with Esther there is only the barest hint of Jewishness, a humorous line of imitative accent: "Vell vy nod? Am I nod mine-self an immi-grunt?" The first mention of Jew in connection with Esther occurs in a description of her house, where Wolfe makes another of his laudatory generalizations about what he most admired in the Jewish nature.

> One of the finest elements in the Jewish character is its sensuous love of richness and abundance: the Jew hates what is savorless and stingy in life, he will not stand for bad food or dreary discomfort, he will not make jokes about them, or feel it a fine thing to cheat the senses. He feels there is something mean and degraded about poor living, he loves warmth and opulence, and he is right.[29]

And the first application of the word "Jewish" to Esther refers to a comic gesture she sometimes makes with her hands, "Jewishly raised her palms to the attendant universe." Esther occasionally uses Jewish dialect for humorous effect as when the fire ended her party, "Vell, ve should have a fire sale!" But such instances are examples of spontaneous good humor and are not intended to deprecate her race. Actually, she is quite proud of her Jewish blood and glories in her Jewish heritage.

When Wolfe wrote that George Webber saw in Esther's face "all the dark opulence of the women of her race" he was subtly invoking an image that is a world-wide sex symbol—the beautiful Jewess. The universal connotation of this image has been commented upon by various writers, one of whom is the French novelist-philosopher and high priest of existentialism, Sartre, who declares: "There is in the words 'a beautiful Jewess' a very special sexual signification, one quite different from that contained in the words 'beautiful Rumanian,' 'beautiful Greek,' or 'beautiful American,' for example." [30] The full import of this universal image was certainly not lost upon Wolfe, whose concern with imagery is everywhere apparent in his work. Coupled with this interest in imagery is the fact that Wolfe was not only a sensuous writer of Keatsian quality but was one of the most sensual writers of his generation. Despite his sensuality and his frank revelations about the George-Esther relationship, Wolfe did exercise some restraint in casting Esther in the role of sex symbol even though to him the Jewess was undeniably a sex symbol.

Wolfe's first mention of a Jewess is as a sex symbol. In Eugene's adolescent fantasy, and one of his numerous Biblical allusions (here to David and Bathsheba) he expresses the desire, "Oh to be king, and see a fruity wide-hipped Jewess bathing on her roof, and to possess her." The "yielding voices of Jewesses" he associates with hen and egg images, timeless and universal symbols of fertility, when he describes Eugene's Jewish students. But the Jewess as sex symbol is best stated by Wolfe himself in one of his most overtly phallic passages.

> The Jewish women were as old as nature, and as round as the earth; they had a curve in them. They had gone to the wailing walls of death and love for seven thousand years, the strong convulsive faces of the Jews were ripe with grief and wisdom, and the curve of the soul of the Jewish women was still unbroken. Female, fertile, yolky, fruitful as the earth, and ready for the plow, they offered to the famished wanderer, the alien, the exile, the baffled and infuriated man, escape and surcease of the handsome barren women, the hard varnished sawdust dolls, the arrogant and sterile women, false in look and promise as a hot-house peach, who walked the streets and had no curves or fruitfulness in them. The Jewish women waited with rich yolky cries for him, and the news they brought him, the wisdom they gave to him was that he need not strangle like a mad dog in a barren dark, nor perish, famished, unassuaged, within the wilderness beside a rusted lance—but that

there was still good earth for the plow to cleave and furrow, deep cellars for the grain, a sheath for the shining sword, rich pockets of spiced fertility for all the maddened lunges of desire.[31]

In making the Jewess a sex symbol Wolfe is thus employing a widely-used image of world literature, and in casting Esther in the Dark Lady motif he is following one of the oldest traditions of the American novel. It is worth noting that the first Jewish character in American fiction was Achsa Fielding in Charles Brockden Brown's *Arthur Mervyn*. Mrs. Fielding, the rich widow whom Arthur marries in preference to the young Eliza Hadwin, prefigures Mrs. Jack in a number of ways: she is Jewish, a wife and mother, older than the hero (six years), wealthy, and diminutive in stature. Although such similarities are but interesting coincidences, Esther does fit into the tradition of sedate and suggested symbol of American fiction rather than the stark symbols which Wolfe's diction makes of the other Jewesses in his books. The reason for this must have been the great love he at one time had for Esther. But despite the palliation of this aspect of Esther Jack, she still remains such a symbol. The universal use of the Jewess as sex symbol has prompted Jewish writers to contradict such an idea. As one recent writer has pointed out, "Traditional Jewish life involved strong defenses against sexual impulses." [32] The truth of such a statement is unquestionable, but Esther Jack's background, as depicted by Wolfe, could hardly be described as traditional Jewish life. In fact Wolfe once wrote in his notebook: "*Esther/* The world of which she was a member was unquestionably a world abnormally marked by corrupt and tainted elements and there can be no doubt that Esther, mature and knowledgeable woman of the world as she indubitably was, was aware of this." [33] Mrs. Jack is a thoroughly emancipated woman, and is therefore free from many traditional Jewish restraints. As a free agent she fulfills many roles in the life of George Webber.

In the capacity of lover, Esther's multi-role function includes that of mistress, cook, mentor, patron, muse, and mother, all of which combined into a tripartite ministration to the heart, body and spirit of George Webber. Seldom in the annals of amour have greater demands been made on mortal woman or have been more willingly and fully met by her. When Wolfe wrote in exultation of Esther "in all the world there was no one like her," his romantic praise embodies a literal truth that would be difficult to dispute. Surely the ghosts of many heroines from Guinevere to Jennie Gerhardt must have curtsied to Esther Jack.

In addition to her role as mistress, Esther also served as cook, not less demanding, for the ravenous George. No writer since Dickens has written more about food than did Wolfe, and Wolfe discusses food as lovingly as many writers do love itself. His diction in connection with food is frequently that which most writers reserve for sex. The explanatory simile that Joel Pierce uses in characterizing Eugene to his sister is appropriate: "When he sees food, he looks as if he's just getting ready to rape a woman!" This quality in Wolfe prompted one critic to label him as perhaps the greediest of American novelists and to write of him, "His craving for food and drink turned into passionate love affairs, making his addresses to apples, lettuce and sirloin steak sound like the ardent perorations of an infatuated man to his mistress." [34] Esther was a fine cook and greatly skilled in the preparation of Jewish dishes, which especially appealed to the Webber taste.

An equally important role of Esther's was in meeting another fundamental need of George—that for a mentor. In *The Story of a Novel* Wolfe elaborated the famed search-for-a-father theme as a quest for "the image of a strength and wisdom external to his need and superior to his hunger, to which the belief and power of his own life could be united." His belief in this idea as the "deepest search in life" not only is enshrined in his book but was enacted in his own life over and over. From his childhood until almost his death Wolfe seized upon one person or another for "strength and wisdom." The list is a familiar one: his brother Ben in childhood, Margaret Roberts in high school, Professor Horace Williams at Chapel Hill, George Pierce Baker at Harvard, Aline Bernstein in New York, and finally Maxwell Perkins. Each of these made important contributions to Wolfe at some juncture of his development, and each was in turn supplanted by the next when a newer need arose. Miss Nowell refers to these people as "father substitutes" but the term can be misleading. It is difficult to find one word which adequately describes the places they filled in the life of Wolfe. Perhaps their function is best described by the Hindu term "guru," but it is probably just as well to use mentor. In any event, a mentor was an absolute necessity to Wolfe, and in his choice of mentors—as in many of the splendid accidents of his life—he was extremely fortunate. These he chose, to whom "the belief and power of his life could be united," were indeed superior people.

As mentor at this point in his life George could hardly have made a better choice than Esther; she was indeed "a brilliant thread in the web of all its dense complexity." The oft repeated source of Esther's strength is her firm belief in a Carlylean doctrine of work. This was her real religion, and from it "all the good things in her life and person came." In bringing order to the chaos of George's life and setting him upon a regular schedule of work Esther made one of her major contributions.

Although there are hints in the fictional account of Esther's role as patron, Wolfe's pride did not permit him to give the full revelation on this point that he does to other aspects of the relationship. However, his notebook entries do reveal his patron's subsidization. While he was abroad writing *Look Homeward, Angel,* for example, he recorded the receipt of money in a terse note: "Wednesday—London Again—Nov. 24, 1926—Food cable and money from my Jew—How shall the years pass Jew?" [35] Despite the growing frequency of their bitter quarrels, the faithful Esther's belief in his ability and her determination for him to realize the best of his talents were unwavering.

Still another facet of Esther's function as lover is that of muse. In Webber's ardent quest for fictive material he found in Esther a rich source, and he mined the lode with the relentlessness of a gold prospector. This drawing on Esther for literary material is minutely described in *The Web and the Rock,* and if Esther became an exhausted muse, it is not surprising because of Webber's efforts to squeeze her dry of literary material.

A fiction writer may write upon one or more of three ascending levels of experience. The first level is that of the experience of the author himself, the material which his own life provides him. The second level is the experience of others, that which the author learns through observation and investigation. The third level, and the one generally conceded to be the highest, is that of pure creation, the working of the author's imagination. Almost all novelists, it would probably not be amiss to say *every* novelist, write at times on the first level. Melville in *Moby Dick,* Dickens in *David Copperfield,* Hawthorne in *The Blithedale Romance,* Charlotte Brontë in *Vilette,* Mark Twain in *Huckleberry Finn,* Hemingway in *A Farewell to Arms* certainly show instances of writing on the fist level. Truly great novelists, however, are not confined to the first level. Dickens employs all three in *David Copperfield,* and in *Huckleberry Finn* Mark Twain plays up and down the scale at will. Hemingway treads heavily on the second level in *The Sun Also Rises,* just as does Melville in *White Jacket.* Few novels hold to the third level with the pristine purity of *The Scarlet Letter,* but *Wuthering Heights* and *The Sound and the Fury* must be cited as classical examples.

Writing on the first level, an author runs the risk of producing autobiography rather than fiction. Since Webber did the great bulk of his writing on the first level, that is the very trap into which he fell. This is not to maintain that fictionalized autobiography is inartistic *per se;* it may be artistry of a high quality, as is exemplified by the works of Proust. But until autobiographical fiction becomes a recognized and accepted genre, Wolfe will continue to be deprecated by critics for his persistence in writing on the first of the three levels. Nevertheless, his great talents enabled him to produce autobiographical fiction of a high merit. The raw material of his own experience did undergo an artistic transmutation that is fully evident in his writing even though actuality was not obscured in the process.

One of Esther's functions as muse was in assisting him to progress from the first to the second level. She not only provided him with literary material but her enthusiasm and zest for that material proved an added stimulus to his using it. Wolfe gives a half page of subjects that Webber pumped from Esther and concludes with the admission that he began to get fixed in his imagination an opulent and thrilling picture of the city in the nineties and early years of the twentieth century. Wolfe's use of some of this material is scattered throughout both of the posthumous novels. His use of the material gained from Esther's experience (for example Chapter 27 of *The Web and the Rock,* "Stein and Rosen's") convinced him that he could successfully write on the second level, and undoubtedly prompted him to continue, especially as he began to deplete the resources of his own experiences. Actually Wolfe did some of his best writing using other people's experiences as fictive material. "Chicamauga," one of his best stories, is based on the experiences of his great-uncle, John Westall, who was ninety-five when he related them to Wolfe in the spring of 1937. His Joycean gem, "The Web of Earth," is based on his mother's endless stream of reminiscences weaving itself into her son's mind. At the time of his death Wolfe had been writing fairly consistently on the second level, as is quite apparent in his unfinished novel, *The Hills Beyond.* Certain passages of this work give indication that he also rose to the third level. However, in all his published writings prior to *The Hills Beyond,* with the exception of such isolated instances as the consummate final chapter of *Look Homeward, Angel* and the stultified "Fame and the Poet," there is little evidence that he attempted sustained writing on the third level. Such occasions are rare and relatively brief.

There remains yet one other facet of Esther's office of lover and it is that of mother. The roles of lover and mother may seem to be mutually exclusive but psychology holds that many a wife fulfills this dual role. So did the versatile Esther. Vardis Fisher in writing his essay, "My Experiences with Thomas Wolfe" (a valuable one despite its being marred by Fisher's all too obvious jealousy of Wolfe's success), makes a telling point: "Anyone who would understand Wolfe must understand his relationship with his mother." While an exploration of that relationship is beyond the scope of this study, it is pertinent to observe that Wolfe was both psychologically and financially dependent upon his mother long beyond the usual time. The fact that Wolfe achieved any real financial independence from his mother before he was thirty is due not so much to his job at New York University as it is to Mrs. Bernstein's supplanting Mrs. Wolfe as banker (until Scribner's took over this function).

However, even more important than the financial aspect was Mrs. Bernstein's assumption of the psychological one also. Mr. Fisher, following Jungian doctrine, observes that Wolfe's mother became a "specter of anxiety" for him. (His choice of Jungian rather than Freudian theory here is an appropriate one.) The psychological scars upon Wolfe made by the divided home in his youth and his childhood longing for attention and affection were deep indeed. Though supplied in part by Margaret Roberts, whom he called "his spiritual mother," these fundamental needs were apparently never fully met until the advent of Aline Bernstein. In providing Wolfe a "home" and in supplanting the "dreaded mother" image with the tender love, affection, and constant attention for which he so desperately yearned, she filled the emotional need for a mother that had never been previously met —not even by Margaret Roberts. All these implications are interwoven into the ministrations of Esther Jack.

Despite Esther's magnificent performance in her hexamerous role of lover there is in the unfolding of the story a mounting disenchantment with her on the part of Webber, and a contributory factor in this alienation is her race. As noted above, there was in the first meeting with Esther only the barest hint of her race and it is not until much later that Wolfe applies the word "Jewish" to Esther. From the point Wolfe introduces Esther into the story until the end of Book IV—except for the interpolated chapter on "Stein and Rosen's"—there are very few references and allusions, even oblique ones, to Esther's race. Book IV is entitled "The Magic Year" and covers the "honeymoon" period of the relationship. It is quite significant that during this period, while Webber remained in an ecstatic state of love, there are so few references to the race of his beloved.

Early in the relationship, despite its golden glow, the first faint cloud of trouble appeared when "he saw the look on her face that he had seen once or twice before on the ship, and which already had power to wound his suspicion and to awake in him a jealous curiosity." This expression of hers which troubles him is not described as Jewish, however, but rather as "almost Slavic." Webber's reaction was that he "felt tricked and cheated and baffled by a cleverness and subtlety of living that was too old, too wise and crafty, for him to fathom or contend with." This ancient wisdom and craftiness will later be labeled as Jewish, but when Webber senses it here, no such label is applied.

During the early part of the relationship it is usually Esther who brings up her race. In describing street scenes to George she tells him that "sometimes there's nothing but the Jews" and adds, "but it's no use telling you and Daddy—you're both Gentiles and you wouldn't know what I was talking about."

The first real hint of trouble, though, is given when Webber remembers a play they had attended because "that night had given him the first sense he had that there was something wrong, for him at least, in their relationship." And immediately after this hint of trouble, references to Esther's race begin to appear. It would seem that there is a subconscious linking in his mind between the wrongness in the relationship and Esther's race. Certainly after the quarrel erupts, as it grows in intensity the racial references increase in an almost mathematical ratio.

Esther defends her race vigorously in verbal battle with George even to the point of equating it with probity and faithfulness while indicting Gentiles as the equivalence of perfidy and disloyalty: "My people are loyal! . . . With us love is a thing that lasts!" and adds sarcastically, "We're not like you fine and noble Christians . . . these great and wonderful Gentiles." After this outburst, harmony is restored for a time but the racial question remains a touchy point. When Esther inquires whom George saw at the publishing firm and he replies "A Jew," she instantly recoils "in an excited and warning tone of voice: 'Now you're beginning again!' " George, however, declares his love for Esther in spite of her "imperfections" and he singles out two for specific mention, one of which is her "racial hysteria." Though he loves her still, her race is becoming an increasingly disturbing element to him.

With the spiritual and mental deterioration that George undergoes, a madness compounded of many elements took possession of him, and his mind concocts a fantastic idea: he sees Esther as the nucleus of a sinister Jewish scheme to entrap him. In this incredible fantasy Wolfe ironically, and perhaps subconsciously, selects an ancient and famous Gentile plot against a noble Jew and reverses it. He pictures Webber as a Gentile Samson caught in a Jewish plot "into which his own folly had led him," and like Samson "he was shorn of his strength forever." Esther thus becomes a Jewish Delilah, an image which heightens the ridiculousness of the situation, and by this inversion of a classic plot Wolfe causes Webber to become a ludicrous rather than the tragic figure he evidently intended him to be.

Wolfe's constant tendency to generalize the individual into the universal is active here also. In his feverish imagination Webber sees his entrapment by Esther not as an isolated instance, but rather it is a part of the gigantic plot of Jewry which imperils every Christian man of genius. In his distorted mind he sees a dark regiment of Jewish women in their lavish beauty serving as bait for the unwary Christian genius. Then, in a rapid mixing of symbolism, these Jewish women are simultaneously a medieval instrument of torture and the supreme symbol of New Testament Christianity, a cross: "They were the living rack on which the trembling backs of all their Christian lovers had been broken, the living cross on which the flesh and marrow of Christian men had been crucified." The man of genius thus becomes both a martyr and a Christ figure, the innocent victim of a wicked plot. The cunning perpetrators of this crime are the descendants of those whose shouts of "Barabbas, Barabbas" sent Christ to the cross, "great, beak-nosed Jews, filled with insolence and scorn, with dark pride and an unutterable patience." In this clever way the Jew wreaks his revenge upon the flower of the Gentiles, the man of genius, in retaliation for the score of centuries of persecution which have followed the crucifixion of Christ.

Wolfe continues in his Biblical strain of imagery by apostrophizing the martyred man of genius as "son of man," Christ's favorite designation of himself. The passage affords an example of juxtaposition of the sacred and profane seldom encountered in the work of a major writer. At the same time he is addressing the "son of man" and invoking Biblical imagery, the questioning sinks to the level of lewdness: "Could she sit on her delicate tail and banter away about the light refinements of adultery?" But Esther is beyond detection. The great network of Jewry closes around her and she is "buried safely . . . at the homes and estates

of rich and sensual Jewish women, who aided and abetted her."
Although Wolfe pictures this whole fantastic scheme (a rework-
ing of the ancient myth) as the product of a diseased mind, nevertheless by focusing upon what, to the Gentile mind, is the arch
example of Jewish villainy, he brands Esther ineradicably as the
daughter of a despised race.

Wolfe represents the course of love (and Webber's relationship
with Esther) as evolving through four stages:

> (1) a young man's exultant pride and vainglory in what he
> thought of as a brilliant personal conquest—the possession of the
> love of a beautiful and talented woman—a tribute to his vanity.
> (2) Then his vanity and joy of sensual conquest gave way to
> the humility and adoration of love, until every pulse, energy, and
> passion of life became obsessed by her.
> (3) . . . the terrible invasions of love which rob men of their
> unshared secrecy. . . . And when he first began to realize the deep
> exclusiveness of love, the extent to which it was absorbing all his
> thoughts and energies, he felt the price he paid for it was too
> exorbitant. . . .
> (4) . . . finally, all the proud, triumphant music of this love
> which had possessed and conquered him was being broken, cor-
> rupted, made dissonant and harsh by these recurring waves of
> doubt, suspicion, hate, and madness. . . .[36]

In the first two stages it had not mattered adversely that Esther
was Jewish, but when the third stage was reached and the disenchantment began, it did matter. In the fourth stage Esther's race
becomes a paramount issue.

The culmination of hatred is recognized by Esther when she
reproaches George, "You've reviled and hated all my people—and
now, I ask you, who's stuck by you, who's been your friend?" The
resulting outburst of bitterness is swallowed by temporary remorse and brief reconciliation, but once hatred has been recognized and labeled by Esther, it is on other occasions repeated:
"You're always reviling us. You couldn't see the truth about us
anyway, you hate us so!" This attitude of George's is reflected in
other ways; the "old and worldly humor of her race" becomes "the
cynical humor of old Jewish scorn," and similar examples could
be multiplied. Thus, in the fourth stage of love, Webber's disenchantment indeed passed through doubt, suspicion, hate, and
madness. The hatred is focused upon Esther as a member of her
despised race. When Webber hurls the supreme insult at Esther it
is, "And you're acting like a Jew! A damned, crafty Jezebel of a
Jew." Esther's role of the Jew as lover has gone full cycle; the term

"Jew" has metamorphosed from one of endearment to that of utter contempt and hatred.

The Jew as Symbol

The final category into which Wolfe's Jewish characters may be grouped is the Jew as symbol. The following discussion is not an abnegation of the symbolic implications of the characters treated above, of course, nor is it a recapitulation of them. Many of Wolfe's characters like Melville's are inherently symbolic and their symbolic significance has been treated in another context. There are, however, three Jewish figures which Wolfe so patently intended as symbols that they do not fit naturally into any of the other categories but necessitate a special designation of their own. They are "the Jew boy," Abraham Jones's mother, and "old Fuss-and-Fidget." Moreover, they constitute symbolic phases of Wolfe's famed concept of time: "actual present time," "past time," and "time immutable."

The most starkly ostensible symbol of the three is "the Jew boy" in Wolfe's patriotic paean "The Promise of America" in *You Can't Go Home Again,* where the erstwhile wanderer reaffirms his vibrant faith in his native land as the promised land of golden opportunity in the spirit of Whitman's *Democratic Vistas.* To demonstrate America as the land where ambition becomes actuality, Wolfe takes his mythical "seeker" and ensconces him in Shelleyan fashion on a vantage point (the Rocky Mountains) for a rapid Queen Mab survey of continental U.S.A. Although Wolfe, as is to be expected, points out choice foods—New York grapes, Georgia watermelons, and Colorado cantaloupes—he directs the seeker's vision to the ambitious youths of the cities, towns, and villages who are burning in the night. From ten thousand places he selects three boys who are representative of racial or regional minorities and in whom ambition burns like fire: a Negro, a Southerner, and a Jew.

The Negro boy from the South Chicago slums seeks fame through physical prowess, prizefighting, in a manner reminiscent of the career of Joe Louis. The descendant of slaves is now a champion; the victory is simultaneously an individual and a racial triumph. The second figure is a lean and tan-faced boy from the clay-baked Piedmont of the South. He too seeks fame through athletic prowess, but his sport is baseball. His rawhide arm and ambition carry him from the sandlots of the South to Yankee

Stadium where he strikes out the mighty Gehrig, the pride of the Yankees, in a triumph that is both personal and regional. The third youth is the "Jew boy" from the East-Side Ghetto of Manhattan. He also thirsts for fame, but unlike the other two, he seeks his fulfillment on the intellectual level.

This "Jew boy" with his "weak eyes squinting painfully through his thick-lens glasses" as an image certainly owes a debt to Abraham Jones. But although a student, he is not individualized, as Michalove, Jones, and Fried are. Wolfe intends him as a racial symbol, and as such he bears the Wolfean hallmark of his race, a "huge beaked nose." As a first generation American, the product of European immigration, he struggles in his cell in the tenement to achieve distinction in the highest realm and is inspired by the most fabled Jew of the twentieth century: "He sees the class, the lecture room, the shining apparatus of gigantic laboratories, the open field of scholarship and pure research, certain knowledge, and the world distinction of an Einstein name." Wolfe places his approval, however, upon the achievement and not the choice of medium.

> So, then, to every man his chance—to every man, regardless of his birth, his shining, golden opportunity—to every man the right to live, to work, to be himself, and to become whatever thing his manhood and his vision can combine to make him—this, seeker, is the promise of America.[37]

Whether it be prize fighting, baseball, or science does not really matter to him; fame in any of these is just as sweet. But it is also obvious that in this trilogy of overt symbols the goal of the Jew is the highest, and Wolfe tacitly bestows upon his race an accolade. By allusion to Einstein he reminds his readers that the most outstanding single contribution made in the twentieth century in the realm of pure intellect was made by a Jew. The "Jew boy" as symbol is thus a tribute to the Jewish race, and it is highly significant that the Jewish seeker strives in the intellectual instead of the financial realm and follows in the footsteps of Einstein rather than those of Otto Kahn. The Negro's path leads through the prize ring, the Southerner's across the diamond, but the Jew's (in Wolfe's shunning the conventional myth) lies not through the market place but in the temple of knowledge.

The "Jew boy" is an instance where Wolfe has taken an individual (Abraham Jones) and by the reverse of his usual process has depersonalized him into an objectified symbol. The symbol therefore becomes the embodiment of a quality which, in Coleridge's well-known words, "partakes of the reality which it renders intelligible." As such, it is a forward-looking symbol which assumed a prophetic forecast of the future even while including the pattern of the past, the transcendent rise from ghetto to fame's pinnacle, and thus is the symbolic correlative of "time immutable."

The second of Wolfe's Jewish symbols is Abraham Jones's mother, but unlike the objectified symbol for which her son was the prototype she is individuated. Mrs. Jones is a Yiddish-speaking Polish immigrant, and the mother of an unusual family. Despite her long residence in New York she remains singularly aloof from the city and has learned only a few mangled words and scraps of English. Her most fully presented attribute is her poignant grief for her son Jacob, who has been dead more than a year when Eugene meets her. Mrs. Jones stands alone from all of Wolfe's other Jewish characters in one important respect; she is religious: "her life was rooted in the soil of two devotions: the synagogue and the home." In these particulars she almost becomes a stereotype of the old immigrant Jewess, but not quite, for Wolfe presents her not as stereotype but as symbol.

Mrs. Jones has "the powerful and primitive features of the aged Jewess" including the Wolfean racial hallmark, "a powerful beaked nose." Although her face was like a worn rock at which all the waves of life had smashed and beaten, it is nevertheless the mark of endurance. To Wolfe "her face might have served . . . as the painting of the whole history of her race," for he viewed it as the outward expression of what her life symbolizes to him—the indestructibility of her race—or, as he further expresses it, "the timelessness of her race and destiny." Even without his explanatory statement, Wolfe's likening her face to a rock, one of his favorite symbols for permanence and fixity, makes clear his symbolic implication. In addition to the general fluidity of life with its innumerable vicissitudes she has undergone transplantation to an alien land whose tongue she never understands, the loss of homeland, separation from her husband, deep and abiding sorrow, privation, and poverty, all that fate can hurl at her, with a patient endurance and fortitude representative of her race. For her, as for her race, "the passing of seven thousand years was like the passing of a single day." She is thus a racial symbol but a backward-looking symbol. Although she spawns a family to insure racial perpetuity, she represents the history rather than the future of her race and is therefore the symbolic correlative of "past time."

Mrs. Jones is significant not only as the one religious Jewish character or as symbol of the indestructibility of her race, but in her delineation Wolfe came as near as he ever did to achieving a true archetypal character or, more properly, an archetypal portrait. Many of his characters, especially his major ones, are bigger than life but do not warrant designation as archetypes. It is evident, however, that Wolfe viewed Mrs. Jones as being of archetypal proportions and so attempted to portray her. Her face "might have served not only as the painting of the whole history of her race, but," he adds with a primordial sweep, "as the painting of the female everywhere . . . the female timeless, ageless, fixed in sorrow and fertility." In singling out these two cosmic feminine qualities, Wolfe quickly abandons his effort at creating a Jewish matriarchal archetype and attempts to portray Mrs. Jones on a grander universal scale as both the sorrowful mother and Earth-mother images. Of the two he is the more successful with the former, although both attempts are failures.

He is genuinely impressed with the old woman's grief for her deceased son, and in typically Wolfean metaphor he compares this grief to the city and finds it "taller than their tallest towers, and more enduring than all their steel and stone." In choosing the theme of maternal grief Wolfe properly selected an archetypal image that goes back not only to the *mater dolorosa* of Christian art but far beyond, back of Thetis of the *Iliad* even, back to Ishtar, "creatress of peoples, 'the fruitful mother who knows lamentation.' " [38] Eugene recognized this grief "as ancient, timeless, and savage as the earth," but he failed to develop it along historic classical lines or even the more obvious Biblical one of "Rachel weeping for her children." But this archetypal opportunity was missed because of Wolfe's self-limiting angle of vision; at that time everything must be reflected in the light of its effect on the center of gravity of his universe, Eugene. Therefore, Wolfe the solipsist smashes an artistic opportunity to pieces with the egocentric line: "it filled him with horror, anger, a sense of cruelty, disgust, and pity."

Immediately following this destructive line, Wolfe turns to the second image, that of Earth-mother, and begins with a lofty tone: "She was the fertile and enduring earth from which they sprung." And her children, although transformed sharply and curiously by the city still are drawn to her with devotion and respect. But seven lines later the Earth-mother image deteriorates into "broodhen of the earth." The short paragraph concludes with the statement of her "two devotions: the synagogues and the home" and the observation that they are the "soil" that "was ageless, placeless, everlasting." Following this paragraph Wolfe goes on to a discussion of Abe's father and Abe's childhood. The Earth-mother image proves but a flash in Wolfe's rhetoric. In this respect, as in other ways, Wolfe was fundamentally a disciple of Whitman, who held an anti-archetypal view of literature.

The third instance of the Jew as symbol occurs in Wolfe's powerful novella, "I Have a Thing to Tell You," first published in *The New Republic* and later included in greatly expanded form in *You Can't Go Home Again*. Here Wolfe gives a straightforward, eyewitness account of a Jewish lawyer's attempt in 1936 to escape from Nazi Germany and of his capture at the border. This man, whom Wolfe dubs "old Fuss-and-Fidget" and gives no other name, is both a specific and a general symbol. Specifically, he is a symbol of the Jewish victims of Nazi brutality, but in a general sense he is representative of man's inhumanity to man.

By setting the unfortunate man's capture within a framework of a generally anti-Jewish German attitude, Wolfe enhances his significance as a Jewish symbol even though he makes Fuss-and-Fidget less Jewish than any of his other Jewish characters. In the first place he lacked the Wolfean hallmark; his nose was a "long nose" but Wolfe, as if to deny the hallmark here, expressly states, "It was not grotesquely hooked and beaked." Though Wolfe goes to some length to individualize Fuss-and-Fidget, he takes pains to give him a non-Jewish appearance. Webber, who is elsewhere alert to any hint of Jewishness, is surprised to learn the man is Jewish. But in accepting the man's racial identity as fact and in placing his tragedy within the given frame of reference Wolfe thereby makes him representative of the persecution inflicted upon the Jews by Nazi Germany.

Wolfe's purpose in contravening his usual practice of making his Jewish characters unmistakably Jewish was evidently that he desired Fuss-and-Fidget to serve not only as a specific symbol but also as a general symbol as well. If Wolfe had too definitely identified him as a Jew in the beginning, it would have weakened him, in Wolfe's mind at least, as a symbol of all mankind. Therefore, Wolfe cloaked him with a non-racial anonymity: "He was just a drab, stuffy, irascible little fellow of the type that one sees a thousand times a day." To be a general symbol Wolfe makes of him a universal type, undistinguished in any of the scores of ways that Wolfe so deftly stamped the hundreds of portraits as vividly individualized from the other members of the human race. Therefore, the man's personal tragedy is not only that of a Jew enmeshed in the cruel Nazi net; he becomes the larger symbol of mankind victimized by evil.

> And the little man—he, too, paused once from his feverish effort to explain. As the car in which he had been riding slid by, he lifted his pasty face and terror-stricken eyes, and for a moment his lips were stilled of their anxious pleading. He looked once, directly and steadfastly, at his former companions, and they at him. And in that gaze was all the unmeasured weight of man's mortal anguish. George and the others felt somehow naked and ashamed, and somehow guilty. They all felt that they were saying farewell, not to a man, but to humanity; not to some pathetic stranger, some chance acquaintance of the voyage, but to mankind; not to some nameless cipher out of life, but to the fading image of a brother's face.[39]

The cogency of this experience resulted in swift resolution of an ideological debate that had been taking place in Wolfe's mind. His romantic attachment to the German past, "the dark, lost Helen that had been forever burning in his blood," is severed by the realization that the Germany of that hour is an infestation of evil. That strong attachment is now ended with finality of the closing of a door. Using evocative Faustian imagery Wolfe bids an emotional farewell to "the other part of his heart's home." This recognition of the true portent of Nazi Germany and its symbolic representation in the implied fate of Fuss-and-Fidget makes of him a symbol of immediacy—the symbolic correlative of "actual, present time."

The full signification of this symbolical interpretation is enhanced in the novella version of "I Have a Thing to Tell You" by the final two paragraphs.

> Something has spoken to me in the night, burning the tapers of the waning year; something has spoken in the night; and told me I shall die, I know not where. Losing the earth we know for greater knowing, losing the life we have for greater life, and leaving friends we loved for greater loving, men find a land more kind than home, more large than earth.
>
> Whereon the pillars of this earth are founded, toward which the spirits of the nations draw, toward which the conscience of the world is tending—a wind is rising, and the rivers flow.[40]

In *You Can't Go Home Again* these two paragraphs appear at the end of the "Credo" as the conclusion of the book. As C. Hugh Holman has correctly observed, "Perhaps the greatest violence ever done a passage by Wolfe was that done the concluding para-

graphs of 'I Have a Thing to Tell You' when they were transferred to the last page of the novel and set in a totally new
context, so that they appear to be a prophecy of his approaching
death." [41] Wolfe most certainly was not writing here of death but
of life—a life that was to be richer and nobler. As he makes
explicit in *You Can't Go Home Again* this experience was both a
loss and a gain, and the gain far outweighed the loss. It meant
breaking with the Germanic past, a "past that holds man's spirit
prisoner" and turning "toward the rich and life-giving soil of a
new freedom in the wide world of all humanity." Furthermore,
the time-phasic correlation of his symbol is emphasized by his
reference to the here and now: "And there came to him a vision of
man's true home, beyond the ominous and cloud-engulfed horizon
of the here and now, in the green and hopeful and still-virgin
meadows of the future." Gone is the time when "his dark roots
. . . could be left to feed upon their own substance and nourish
their own little self-absorbed designs." This statement is an indication that Wolfe's angle of vision has shifted outward and he sees
the dignity of the individual not in terms of Eugene-George but in
the broader terms of the individual worth "of all humanity," an
acknowledgment of the brotherhood of man. The "priceless meas-
ure of his gain," therefore, is to be found through sacrifice (losing
life and friends for "greater life" and "greater loving") and
growth ("losing the earth we know for greater knowing"). It is
the brotherhood of man that Wolfe sees as a bedrock truth
("whereon the pillars of his earth are founded"), as a spiritual
magnet ("toward which the spirits of the nations draw"—a phrase
deleted in *You Can't Go Home Again*), and the attainable ideal
("toward which the conscience of the world is tending"). Thus,
in the final analysis, Wolfe is here espousing the Shelleyan concept of the perfectibility of man.

The Clue to an Enigma

All his life Thomas Wolfe was acutely conscious of the presence
of Jewish blood in the people he met, and he regarded them not
just as individuals but rather as Jews. In his notes preparatory for
his writing, observations, impressions, and resumés of his actual
experiences he used the racial designation as invariably as he
affixed it to the Jewish characters in his fiction. When he jotted
down among his boyhood memories the violent actions of a neighbor, the neighbor's name is not given; he is simply "The Jew who

shot at his wife on Woodfin Street through the glass." [42] In recording an evening spent with a chance acquaintance in Vienna,
Wolfe refers to the man as an "American Jew from Baltimore,"
not just an American or a man from Baltimore. And during his
stay in Paris in 1930 when he interrupted his journal writing for a
date, he made the notation: "Meeting the pretty Jewess Rita Vale
at three o'clock—More later." [43]

None of Wolfe's fictional characters differ in race from their
prototypes, except Nebraska Crane, because Wolfe gave serious
consideration to racial *ethos* in projecting his characters. In January 1930 he was considering the creation of a character similar to
Rabelais' Friar John of the Funnels, the lusty and robust companion of Gargantua and Pantagruel. Characteristically, he thought
first of the nearest prototype to his projected character that he
knew about, who happened to be Mrs. Bernstein's uncle. Then he
considered making the character "a complete Jew," but on pon-
dering the Jewish *ethos* he rejected the idea of a Jew for such a
Rabelaisian character.

The creation of a figure like Friar John of the Funnels

Who shall stand for the Earth (Eugene-Antaeus)
Could he be Aline's uncle in Hartford? Or shall it be a complete
Jew?
  No—must have Anglo-Teutonic earthiness
Or shall he be a tobacco man (like Buck Duke)?
Better perhaps from among Olin's crowd.[44]

While these notes show his searching for a prototype to fit the
pattern which he has in his mind, they also reveal his concern
with *ethos*. In fact, when Wolfe set out to grapple with abstractions his mind usually turned to individuals whom he felt exemplified the abstractions he wished to set forth. While he was in
Rouen in 1930 he began a delineation which he entitled "On the
Jews." But his thoughts turned homeward and he recalled an
individual Jew he knew back in New York, so that his first remarks "On the Jews" were: "He now remembered often the little
Jew who ran the tailor shop on Fifteenth street, and he thought of
the man with warmth and tenderness, of the pleasanter Jew's-
rhythm of his voice: 'Iss not de little voman who comes in here
your vi-eff?' " [45] In the same manner when he attempted the task
on another occasion he thought of the one he knew best and after
a personal evaluation made another of his absurd generalizations
on Jews: "The Jews: Why is Aline a great Jew—Because she does

not think she has a great mind. Emotionally and psychically they are the most interesting people on earth—intellectually they are sawdust and ashes." [46] That he certainly found them interesting and also useful as fictive material no one can deny.

Wolfe once planned to portray an intellectual Jewish aesthete turned economist and he selected as his prototype Harold Loeb, who had already sat for a famed fictional portrait—that of Robert Cohn in Hemingway's *The Sun Also Rises*. In an unfinished fragment, "1930 (The Return to Egypt)," [47] Wolfe set out to give an account of the problems facing the men of Joyner's class, largely those resulting from the collapse of the economic system. However, in a digression typical of those in which some of his well-known portraits first appear in his notes, he gives a summary of "Levenson's career." Levenson is a rich Jew who went to Princeton, was embittered by it, and has become "the champion of civil liberties and of human rights (if there be any left)." Wolfe says that Levenson went to Princeton because "in poetic phrase, the ass of his inferiority hungered for the kick of scorn." But despite Levenson's manifold activities since Princeton, Wolfe indicates he would have remained largely unknown "if Claude Bulheaver had not written the book about him." Just how Wolfe intended to relate "Levenson's career" to the collapse of the economic system is not clear, as the sketch remained unfinished, but the title is symbolic and a Biblical allusion.

The most obvious fact about Wolfe's presentation of the Jew, however, is that his portrayal is inconsistent and contradictory. There is in it an admixture of admiration, rising at times to love, and of dislike, sinking on occasion to hatred. On the whole, it reflects a paradoxical attitude and betrays a wide range of ambivalence. These antagonistic extremes were never more vividly indicated by Wolfe than when he wrote that George Webber stared at Esther Jack "with bloodshot eyes, in which the fires of love and hate . . . flared instantly together in one joined flame." Sometimes the Jew is seen in the light of one fire, sometimes of the other, but always with an intensity for which fire is an appropriate symbol.

There is much that Wolfe found to admire in the Jewish nature. The qualities of "richness, color, and humor" were ones that he especially liked. Courage was one of the chief virtues to Wolfe and he greatly respected it in any of its manifestations, whether it be the physical courage of Barney Jones, the moral courage of Fried, or the spiritual courage of Mrs. Jones. The patient endurance and racial indestructibility also merits his esteem, although at times it gave him a sense of frustration when he compared it to the transitoriness of one life, his own. The Jewish endowment of and appreciation for intellectuality are characteristics that Wolfe everywhere in his fiction (if not in his notes) praises in strong, encomiastic terms; his admiration for these qualities is, in fact, one of the few consistencies in his delineation of the Jew.

Wolfe's greatest admiration, though, was for what he deemed an innate capability of the Jewish nature, a sensuous enjoyment of abundant living. To him this was the quintessence of the Hebraic superiority over the Gentile way of life. It was the basis for his thorough approval of Mr. Rosen and his praise of the Jews as "the most lavish and opulent race on earth." The ability to gain wealth is considered by most Gentiles as one of the chief Jewish characteristics and is frequently the point of adverse Gentile criticism. It is especially noteworthy that Wolfe not only does not condemn this attribute but thoroughly approves it. While he may occasionally question the means of acquiring wealth, wealth legitimately earned and subsequently enjoyed accounts for some of his most lavish praise.

Another quality that Wolfe admired in the Jew is the strong Jewish sense of family. Although this facet is only adumbrated in his work it is nonetheless present and real. And like his admiration for Jewish lavish living it comes from what he felt he lacked in his own childhood. Certainly the disunity of Wolfe's own family is apparent enough in his works to make his yearning for strong family ties understandable. The tendency of the surviving members of his family to close ranks after he became famous does not obscure the sharp cleavages that existed during his childhood.

Thus, in his panoramic portrayal of the Jew, Wolfe found much to admire, and in his honesty bestowed praises upon what he liked just as he heaped ridicule upon what he disliked. It is well to remember that all of Wolfe's writing except his plays comes after his friendship with Aline Bernstein; *Look Homeward, Angel* was written during his association with her and all the others after the affair was concluded. Since that experience was one of the greatest in Wolfe's entire life, it is hardly conceivable that he viewed the Jew in quite the same light that he would have, had he never loved a Jewish woman. Whether Wolfe's depiction of the Jew is softened because of his love for Mrs. Bernstein is difficult, if not impossible, to ascertain. But it does seem likely that his association with her might have given him insight into the Jewish character he would otherwise not have had. In any event,

Wolfe did see qualities that he admired, and in his characteristic frankness clearly demonstrated that admiration.

However, there is another and darker side of the coin; Wolfe found much to dislike about the Jew. One thing he disliked is what he considered a "Jewish appearance," and in subscribing to the theory of the "Semitic nose" as a racial characteristic he made that organ a target of caricature. It cannot be denied that the term "beak nosed Jew" is a favorite expression of his or that he intended it as derogatory, though he uses other degrading terms sparingly. Arrogance and aggressiveness, however, are traits that he strongly dislikes and considers racial, especially in the characterization of Abe Jones and Fried. Indeed, in the overall pattern of his Jewish characters and in random remarks about urban Jews he treats these two attributes as racial traits. Although Wolfe's Jewish characters are, for the most part, too strongly individuated to be considered stereotypes, in these aspects he betrays Gentile prejudice and approaches the common Gentile stereotype of the Jew.

He viewed any effort by a Jew to conceal his racial origin as opprobrious, and his denunciation of name changing as an effort at racial disguise is quite harsh. It is this attitude which places Wolfe in a position that is both insular and logically untenable. On the one hand he vigorously condemns the Jew for his lack of acculturation, and on the other he berates the Jew for exhibiting evidence of acculturation. It is this same lack of logic that has confronted the Jew in America on nearly every hand, regardless of whether he be recent immigrant or "old" resident.

4 The Foreigner:

'The People of the New America'

Just as Thomas Wolfe was cognizant of racial origin, so was he sensitive to national origin. Persons of recent immigrant stock were as different in their way as were the Negro and the Jew, and these differences find widespread expression in his writing. Not only did Wolfe fulfil Howells' dictum that American novelists "be as American as they unconsciously can," but he was also as consciously an American writer as Whitman. Wolfe's background and temperament combined to produce an Americanism as solid as that of any nineteenth-century patriot, and thereby provided the old-fashioned touchstone by which he judged all who came within his ken.

South of the Border Latins

Wolfe takes little notice of Latin Americans in his fiction. He did not treat any Central or South Americans although he had occasional contact with them. On his third trip to Europe he wrote in his notebook, as was his custom, his impressions of fellow passengers aboard the *George Washington,* and these notes include terse comments on a Nicaraguan: "The little Nicaraguan on this boat—dirty little fellow, insolence and surility—show off." [1] Such notebook jottings frequently emerge later as fictional portraiture, but the little Nicaraguan does not reappear in Wolfe's writing. The sole Cuban he includes, a student at the

Leonard School in Altamont, is accorded only a brief mention when Wolfe merely notes his presence and his different cultural heritage: "the rich Cuban boy, Manual Quevado, whose fat dark laughter and broken speech was all for girls. He belonged to a richer South, but they knew him."

Neither does Wolfe deal with Mexicans in his published works, though they are included in his unpublished manuscripts. In his notes for "O Lost" he gives a young boy's superpatriotic attitude in which the individual fighting ability of a Mexican is well below an Englishman's and far below an American's: "the history we read later—The Liberty boys of '76—'The Red Coats'—One American good as three Englishmen—seven Mexicans." [2] He also wrote a short piece (five typed pages) entitled "The Mexicans" which he intended for "The Hound of Darkness," but Aswell rejected it. In a roadside vignette Wolfe depicts two drunken Mexicans, Pete and Joe, who have wrecked their car in a deep arroyo between Lamy and Santa Fe, New Mexico, but have miraculously escaped unhurt. They are discovered by a passing physician, Dr. Ferguson, who stops to render aid. When the doctor finds that their friend Gus is dead in the wrecked car, Pete and Joe become exultant that, though Gus is dead, "We no hurt!" The two Mexicans are completely devoid of any remorse for the death of their companion; their only reaction is a stupid glee over their own escape. [3] In this brief treatment of Mexicans, Wolfe does not present them as possessing even ordinary human sensibilities.

However, he does have one sympathetic character whom he portrays as having Mexican blood, although this fact was obscured by editorial revision. In *Look Homeward, Angel* one of Eugene's best friends is George Graves, who accompanies him on his famed walk through the town in Chapter XXIV. The published characterization of George Graves contains only the barest hint of Mexican blood; he is addressed twice as "Villa," but even this nickname is not sufficient grounds for suspecting him of being part Mexican since no other reference to him carries any such imputation at all.

The walk-through-the-town sequence, as Wolfe originally wrote it, was about twice as long as it appears in *Look Homeward, Angel*, but Perkins counseled reducing it to its present length. Included in the excised material are all the references to George Graves' Mexican blood except the two instances of his nickname. Not only is Graves regularly called "Villa" by his schoolmates, but he is also sometimes taunted by them about his Mexican ancestry. Wolfe describes his reaction to such a taunt: "George Graves lifted his huge Mexican face sullenly. His black eyes glittered murderously, he seemed ready to burst into tears. His face was contorted indecisively with a bitter sneering smile." [4] While George Graves is embarrassed by his Mexican blood, he makes a conscious effort to conform to the mores of his Anglo-Saxon peers and thereby win their approval, as Wolfe shows in the following description.

> George Graves was sixteen, he was just under six feet and weighed 190 pounds. He was not merely ponderous: he had the strength of an ox. He could have broken the neck of a big man in his hands—he was afraid of his vast strength, afraid of his murderous temper, painfully sensitive to his Latin coloring, and morbidly obedient to the good blonde code of Saxon sportsmanship. His life was full of arrested gestures: murderous, but incomplete movements against his tormentors. [5]

In some instances the references to Graves are simply omitted with little change in the scene. For example, a question of Ralph Rolls in the manuscript is directed to both Eugene and George Graves:

> Ralph Rolls spat with grown-up gusto, and wiped his mouth.
> "What say, Jule?" he asked. "Shall we sing our song for Hal and the Greaser?" [6]

But in the book the question becomes simply, " 'Shall we sing our little song for Handsome Hal?' said Ralph Rolls to his copesmate Julius." The net result of these editorial changes is to depict George Graves as just another ordinary Altamont boy and to remove from Wolfe's fiction his one Mexican character along with its attendant portrayal of the typical American attitude of Mexican inferiority.

Thus the exclusion of Mexicans from Wolfe's published work is due to the editorial blue pencils of Perkins and Aswell and not to intentional omission on the part of the author. While the brief mention of a solitary Cuban remains his sole treatment of Latin Americans in his published work, Wolfe recognized the Latin Americans as a significant element in the melting pot and attempted to portray them in his panorama. The action of his editors, however, did serve to protect him from additional charges of Anglo-Saxon snobbery since he reveals the prevalent attitude of that time toward Latin Americans as being among the lesser breeds that have not contributed significantly to the greatness of America.

European Nordics

Quite naturally the Europeans are the largest group of nationalities dealt with by Wolfe, though some Asiatics are included in his portraits. Wolfe, of course, does not attempt any systematic ethnological study in his fiction, although he is usually interested in determining the *ethos* of any group which he is momentarily engaged in portraying. Since his writing in general reflects different attitudes towards northern and southern Europeans, these two groups of nations are discussed separately.

The British Isles, whence his maternal ancestors came, naturally interested Wolfe and he depicts English, Scotch, and Irish in his books, but no Welsh; of the three the English receive the scantiest treatment. This paucity does not result from willful omission or prejudicial neglect, but rather is due to the fact that the Englishman in America most nearly approximates the American in customs and mores, is the most rapidly assimilated of all foreigners, and is indistinguishable in appearance and, for the most part, in behavior. The traits and features of which Wolfe was particularly observant were simply not as apparent in the English as they were in other nationalities. Wolfe, however, was very conscious of his English ancestry; he once wrote Perkins, "I am an American but I have more English blood in me than the English royal family." And the great English contributions to America—language, literature, government, and law—are of course generally assumed by Wolfe but, with the exception of the literature (to which he was devoted), are seldom commented upon directly.

In *Look Homeward, Angel* Wolfe makes the progenitor of the Gant family an "Englishman named Gilbert Gaunt, which he later changed to Gant," but the family is depicted as thoroughly American. This portrayal of Eugene's paternal relatives provides another interesting sidelight on Wolfe. In shunting aside his paternal grandfather, Jacob Wolf, and replacing him with an Englishman, Wolfe was attempting to provide Eugene with a simon-pure Anglo-Saxon ancestry; Wolfe's fear that Jacob Wolf may have possessed Jewish blood was quite real at the time he wrote *Look Homeward, Angel*.

Gilbert Gant is a man of grandiose speech and his son Oliver is a lover of rhetoric, but Oliver's rhetoric is more reminiscent of the

antebellum South than of ancestral England. Oliver's characterization, despite the fact that he is half English, does not present
him as an Anglophile; on the contrary, he delights in the favorite
American custom of criticism of the English.

Eliza Gant, too, is fully aware of her English ancestry, though
her characterization pictures her as far more Scotch than English.
In "The Web of Earth" when she tells Eugene of her desire to
visit Europe, the first country she lists is "England, where all our
folks came from." But her blood tie with England is considerably
more remote than her husband's; she says her family are all
descended from "the son of that Englishman that came there back
in Revolutionary days to sink those copper shafts out there in
Yancey." Eliza also voices the familiar American myth about
ancestral wealth in England awaiting American claimants.

In *The Web and the Rock* Wolfe uses this idea of the American
claimant to English wealth to satirize pretentiousness. The father
of one of George Webber's friends is a bandy-legged, little Englishman who tried to impress Libya Hill by making such claims in
order to disguise his cockney background, but indignation and
excitement stripped the mask of pretense off Mr. Potterham when
a Negro's dog killed the Potterham's bulldog. In his wrath Mr.
Potterham reveals himself as he really is.

> No longer the great gentleman now, no longer the noble descend-
> ant of the Dukes of Potterham, no longer the blood-cousin of
> belted lords and earls, the possible claimant of enormous titles
> and estates in Gloucestershire when the present reigning head
> should die—but Cockney Potterham now, little Potterham minus
> all his aitches, little Potterham the dealer in nigger real estate and
> the owner of nigger shacks, indomitable little Potterham forget-
> ting all his grammar in the heat and anger of the moment.[7]

Potterham's wife does not appear in the published work, but
Wolfe did intend to include her. In a list of characterizations
which he prepared for "Spangler's Paul" there is a preliminary
sketch of Mrs. Potterham.

> *Mrs. Potterham,* a little gentle, ruddy-faced Englishwoman, who
> in England would belong to the lower middle class. Devoted,
> motherly, so domestic that she hardly leaves the house twice a
> year. Meekly adores her husband, her children. Has none of her
> husband's pretensions to great family and noble birth, keeps tea
> brewing all day long and when the little man flies off the handle,
> is angry or exhausted, out of sorts, says " 'ere now, Charlie, do sit
> down and 'ave a nice 'ot cup of tea." [8]

Aswell used much of the material in this list of characterizations in Chapter 6 of *The Web and the Rock* though he did omit Mrs. Potterham. Obviously Wolfe intended to portray Mrs. Potterham as a foil to her husband's aristocratic pretentiousness.

There is but one instance of a true representative of the English aristocracy: the portrait of John William Macpherson Marriott, the youngest son of an ancient family of the English nobility, is given in *Of Time and the River*. Marriott is married to the great heiress, Virginia Willets, and they live on her ninety-thousand-acre estate near Altamont in the great mansion which her father built. His portrait almost becomes the American stereotype of the aristocratic Englishman: reserved, aloof, crisp, hard-drinking, mustached, and bald. But Wolfe is not drawing upon a stereotype; as usual he fashioned the character from a live model. Marriott's prototype is John Francis Amherst Cecil, the first husband of Cornelia Vanderbilt, and a member of the noble Cecil family which has been prominent in England since Tudor times. A one-time member of the British Foreign Service, he resided at Biltmore House after his marriage until his death in 1955, even though he and Cornelia had long been divorced. In the portrayal of Marriott, Wolfe passed up an opportunity to picture him as another common type in American fiction—the fortune-hunting English aristocrat.

Wolfe was proud of his English heritage, but his pride did not express itself in Anglomania. Although he had opportunity to know Englishmen in Asheville,[9] he made little use of the English as fictive material. His principal references to English traits are in pointing out those he condemned; his approval is usually expressed by implication. But on occasion he would commend an Englishman's action, as he did that of the English actor Louis Calvert: "He was an Englishman, but he loved America so well that he took naturalization papers." Undoubtedly the English trait that Wolfe most esteemed was rapid Americanization.

When Wolfe writes about the Scotch, however, he is more positive and commendatory than he is in dealing with the English.[10] Of the three basic national stocks which constitute the Catawban, it is the Scotch strain that is dominant in appearance and character, especially among the mountaineers.

> Their character has strong Scotch markings: they are cautious and deliberate, slow to make a radical decision. They are great talkers, and believe in prayer and argument. . . . They are perhaps the most immensely conservative people on earth, they reverence authority, tradition, and leadership, but when committed to any de-

cision, they stick to it implacably, and if the decision is war, they
will fight to the end with the fury of maniacs.[11]

Thus it is essentially the Scotch heritage which distinguished, in
Wolfe's mind, the Catawban from other Southerners: "Where the
more fiery South Carolinian or Mississippian will fly into a rage
and want to fight the man who doubts his word or questions his
opinion, the eye of the Catawban begins to glow with a fire of
another sort—the lust for debate, a Scotch love of argument."
Scotch traits are deemed virtues by Wolfe, and the Catawban is a
better man because he possesses them to a marked degree.

Wolfe was acutely conscious of his Scotch blood and ascribes
some of Eugene Gant's characteristics, especially his preternatural
power, directly to his Scotch inheritance. He does not develop the
personality of his maternal grandmother; in *Look Homeward,
Angel* he simply refers to her as "Eliza's mother, a plain worn
Scotchwoman." But in Eliza's case he explicitly defines the source
of much of her remarkable power as "her clairvoyant Scotch
soul," and this unusual trait is passed on to Eugene: "He heard
the ghostly ticking of his life; his powerful clairvoyance, the wild
Scotch gift of Eliza, burned inward back across the phantom years,
plucking out of the ghostly shadows a million gleams of light."
The importance of this wild Scotch gift is enormous, for Wolfe
makes clairvoyant memory the key to Eugene's personality and
the source of much of his literary power.

In his characterization of Eliza, Wolfe gives her numerous traits
which are historically associated with the Scotch, among them are
canniness, frugality, calmness, a tendency to brood, and clannish-
ness. Eliza's canniness is especially apparent in her real estate
operations, an aspect which Wolfe acknowledges in fiction and in
actuality. In 1925 he wrote Professor Homer A. Watt: "My
mother is a very extraordinary woman in her middle sixties,
small, strong, intensely vigorous, and uncannily canny in business
affairs: she is part Scotch." Another equally Scotch characteristic
is frugality, and Eliza's frugality, which extends even to parsimon-
iousness, is legendary; she is depicted as an Aberdonian among
the Caledonians. Actually Mrs. Wolfe grew up during the harsh
years of Reconstruction and the penury of her youth could well
explain her frugality, as indeed Wolfe acknowledges, but in his
subsequent characterization of Eliza the Scotchness of her nature
better accounts for her thrift than does her impoverished youth.
Eliza's Scotch heritage, however, is by no means of recent origin as

her forebears had arrived in America during Colonial days. Native Scots, thirty of whom were residing in Asheville in 1910, are fewer on Wolfe's pages.

Though Wolfe deals mostly with persons of Scotch extraction rather than those of more recent Scottish origin, he makes a conscious effort to determine the Scottish *ethos,* and he obviously admired the Scotch-Americans and lauds the contributions which they have made to the American character. He felt this influence and portrays it in his region, his neighborhood, his church, and in his own family. He presents his autobiographical protagonist as the possessor of the Scotch traits of vitality, endurance, love of argument, clairvoyance, and proclivity for brooding; the Scotch traits of caution, deliberation, and calmness he most definitely did not inherit.

In sharp contrast to the deep admiration for the Scotch is a virulent hatred of the Irish. Although he liked the Irish he knew in Asheville, during his years in Boston he developed an abiding animosity toward the Irish which remained throughout his life and was expressed in some of his bitterest satire, denunciations, caustic comment, and incidental slurring remarks that are scattered through all his books except his first and that become at times pure invective.

Look Homeward, Angel is not only singularly free of anti-Irish bias but also devoid of any Irish characters. Although there are people mentioned in the book whose names indicate they may be of Irish extraction, Wolfe nowhere affixes the national label, a practice he follows in characterizing other nationalities and the Irish elsewhere. Since the Irish-born who were living in Asheville in Wolfe's youth actually outnumbered the Scottish-born (thirty-seven Irish, thirty Scots) and Wolfe knew some of them, the omission of Irish characters from the Altamont panorama in *Look Homeward, Angel* appears to be deliberate.

Eugene Gant's fondness for the Altamont Irish is shown only in retrospect after he encounters the Boston Irish, whom Wolfe caricatures in his portrait of the Murphy family as "a typical family of the Boston Irish." This family portrait finally erupts into a denunciation of the Boston Irish which is as vitriolic as any he ever wrote.

> He despised them: he loathed them because they were dull, dirty, and dishonest, because their lives were stupid, barren, and ugly, for their deliberate and insolent unfriendliness and for the conspiratorial secrecy and closure of their petty and vicious lives,

entrenched solidly behind a wall of violent and corrupt politics and religious fanticism, and regarding the alien, the stranger, with the hostile and ignorant eyes of the peasant.[12]

Living amid such a despicable people, Eugene cannot forget the Altamont Irish, "The wild, extravagant and liberal creatures of his childhood," who seemed to belong to a "grander and completely different race." In explaining the difference Wolfe's anti-urban bias is clear: the Altamont Irish have been nurtured on "the glory of earth and air and sky" while the Boston Irish have "withered upon the rootless pavements, soured and sickened in the savage tumult of the streets, grown hard and dead and ugly in the barren land."

Wolfe's interest in the contrast between the Altamont Irish and Boston Irish continued. Originally his discussion of this difference was much longer in the manuscript of *Of Time and the River* but most of it was cut. Later Wolfe reassembled this excised material into a chapter called "The Old Red Irish" and placed it in the manuscript which he delivered to Aswell. He indicated in his rough outline that it was to be in the "Part I, The Hound of Darkness," but Aswell did not include "The Old Red Irish" in Wolfe's posthumous books. The title Wolfe selected indicates that his attitude toward the Boston Irish had not changed at the time of his death.

"The Old Red Irish" is a forty-four page typescript that is composed of three separate manuscripts put together but no attempt has been made to integrate the material. The title is evidently intended to convey more than the idea of Irish coloring for Wolfe states of the Irish: "They could come in with red hairy hands still reeking with the filth of loot, the blood of murder, the betrayal of their office, and piously deplore the lack of other good Americans such as they." After giving a vehement denunciation of the Irish in general, Wolfe then proceeds to give accounts of Irish people that Eugene knew and liked before he went to Harvard.

In making his attack on the Boston Irish through the Murphy family, Wolfe does not attempt to give all the bases of his charges. He does portray their "insolent unfriendliness," but he only suggests "religious fanaticism" and gives no evidence for "corrupt politics" beyond simply stating that Jimmy Murphy has a clerical position in the Boston City Hall. For the most part his attack is an emotional outpouring of accumulated impressions and grievances of his years in Boston. He does individuate the several members of the family, and he does not resort to stereotypes in his portrayal of the Murphys.

The scorn of the Irish, though, is not confined to the living, for he also expresses contempt for a dead Irishman. In "Death the Proud Brother" he describes the deaths of four men, the first three —an Italian peddler, a professional bum, and a construction worker—all meet violent deaths and Wolfe shows varying degrees of compassion for them. The fourth death is that of a "corrupted cipher" who dies of natural causes in a subway station; he is "unmistakably Irish—city-Irish," and no compassion is felt for him. Wolfe ponders the man's occupation and gives a list of jobs he might have held, all unflattering ones, and suggests that the dead man was probably a "question-evader from some Irish politician, schooled to vote dutifully for 'the boys' upon election day, and to be flung his little scrap of patronage for service rendered and silence kept." This leads Wolfe into a condemnation of Irish politicians and of their hangers-on, whose lives are shaped by "the smell of the boss, the word of the priest, the little spare approvals of Mike, Mary, Molly, Kate, and Pat."

Wolfe's best known portrait of a real Irishman is his excellent satire of Ernest Boyd as "Seamus Malone." Boyd, the husband of Wolfe's first agent, was an Irish-born critic and author whose iconoclastic views are expressed in various of his books, especially *Literary Blasphemies* (1927). Malone is set forth as an arrogant intellectual who denounces the American scene with Menckenian tone and vigor and demolishes a host of contemporary authors; his scathing attack on T. S. Eliot is surpassed only by his acid remarks on James Joyce. Malone is not pictured as devoid of charm; his voice is magnificently full-bodied with Celtic richness and he has a winning smile, but the chief impression Wolfe gives of Seamus Malone is that of an egotistical, Irish, self-appointed literary pontifex whose views are shaped by enormous conceit and swayed by overwhelming prejudice. An Irish literateur, iconoclastic though he may be, is no more appealing to Wolfe than other Irish, whether they hail from Boston or "the remotest purlieus of Brooklyn."

The most moderate of Wolfe's satires on the Irish is his essay "On Leprechauns" which is Horatian in tone, a contrast to the Juvenalian quality he usually displays in writing about the Irish. This essay, which Aswell published as a separate sketch in *The Hills Beyond*, had originally been Wolfe's introduction to his portrait of Seamus Malone. The fact that the Malone portrait was intended for the *New Yorker* may account for the urbane, sophisticated Horatian quality of "On Leprechauns." Wolfe's main purpose in this essay is to contrast the adulation given to any Irish writer who comes to America with the neglect accorded to native son authors, regardless of their individual abilities. But he also takes occasion to include the Irish proclivity for politics.

> Where else in the world may a people be found who will so cheerfully and uncomplainingly take over the onerous and thankless burden of running the government, and whose devotion to the principles of law and order, sobriety, reasonable conciliation, and selfless and unseeking consecration to the common weal are as high, loyal, and untarnished in their idealism as are those of the Irish? [13]

Even while writing in the guise of good-natured satire with the purpose of chiding his own country for neglecting its native writers, Wolfe cannot keep from deriding one of his favorite targets.

He is unusually consistent in maintaining his prejudicial presentation of the Irish, especially the urban Irish. He does not take pains, however, to indicate whether his characters are of recent immigration or the products of long residence in America. The Irish are always alien, undesirable ones at that, whose chief traits are arrogance, cruelty, dishonesty, political corruption, and religious bigotry. Not only have they failed, in Wolfe's view, to contribute anything worthwhile to America, but even America has not been able to bring about any visible improvement in the Old Red Irish of its urban centers.

Wolfe felt there was a "fatal and corrupt dualism of the Irish character." This dualism, as he expresses it in "The Old Red Irish," is the result of "the revolting confluence of a brutal and callous criminality of the soul with the most extravagant excesses of a maudlin sentimentality," and the combination of the two "makes the stench of them intolerable." In his ceaseless search for the symbolic significance of his own experience, Wolfe saw the Irish as emblematic of the darker side of mankind's own flawed character.

> The Irish, then, were not so much an evil and corrupted race as the reflection of our own defeat, a sordid evidence of our own betrayal, the concrete image of our faithless and dishonorable surrender. A curse was on them as it was all of us. In every evil conquest they had added to their own disgrace. In every obscene victory they had added to the full measure of their own defeat, and in the huge finality of their brutal, evil, and corrupted authority, the loss and desolation of their own lives was ruinously apparent.[14]

Since his paternal ancestry was German, and throughout most of his life Wolfe displayed a strong spiritual and cultural affinity for Germany, plus the fact that one of the three main stocks of North Carolina was German, it might reasonably be expected that his works would include a large number of German characters. But they do not. In his two pictures of his father, Wolfe does present him as of German blood: W. O. Gant is portrayed as half-German, and John Webber is of Pennsylvania Dutch extraction but Webber is shown only by portraiture, and he is a pale reflection of Gant. W. O. Gant, one of Wolfe's greatest creations, is a real, tremendously vital character whose gusto makes him a memorable addition to American fiction. Gant, however, is portrayed as thoroughly American and Wolfe nowhere labels any of his traits as German, as he does in identifying certain of Eliza's traits as Scotch.

Although the number of German-born persons in Asheville was forty-eight, a larger group than either the Scotch or the Irish, German characters in *Look Homeward, Angel* are scarce. There are a number whose names indicate German extraction, but Wolfe identifies only three as German: Otto Krause, Stephen Rheinhart, and Margaret Lutz. In 1926 when he began preparing his notes for the writing of *Look Homeward, Angel* he scribbled among his reminiscences, "Speak of Walter Krause, the long-limbed German boy, with the large nose, and soft white hair on his face." Walter does make two appearances in the book as "Otto Krause, a cheese-nosed, hair-faced, inch-browed German boy," who adds little to the narrative. He is purely an individual and not intended to typify anything Germanic, although it is interesting that sixteen years later Wolfe still thought of him as a "German boy."

A schoolmate of an entirely different stripe is Eugene's friend Stephen "Pap" Rheinhart who attended the Altamont Fitting School and is of German extraction. Wolfe was fond of "Pap" and wrote approvingly of him and his family: "He had a gruff voice; he was full of rough kindly humor, and chewed tobacco constantly. His father was wealthy. He lived on a big farm in the Cove, ran a dairy and had a foundry in the town. They were unpretending people—German stock." The Rheinharts are typical of Wolfe's general attitude toward the German-Americans; as stable, hard-working people they make fine citizens and even though they become prosperous they remain unpretentious.

The third German character, Margaret Lutz, is not an Altamont native but came from Indiana as a summer boarder at Dixieland. After her father died and left her some money, Steve Gant, Eugene's oldest brother, married her, although she was

twelve years his senior. Wolfe does not indicate whether she is of
recent German origin or not, but his almost invariable use of the
adjective "German" indicates that she is. He does present her as
having a rather stupid stolidity that he deemed was also characteristic of some Germans, even though her portrait is an individuated one.

When Wolfe transfers his setting away from Asheville his German characters are no more numerous than in *Look Homeward,
Angel.* Although there are many whose names indicate German
extraction, Wolfe tags only three as German; two of these came
from Mrs. Bernstein's experience rather than his own, and the
third is her cook. Esther Jack, in reminiscing of her girlhood,
recounts her visits to the builder of the Brooklyn Bridge and the
great actor Richard Brandell, both of whom were friends of her
father.

The builder of the Brooklyn Bridge is referred to only as "the
man who built the Bridge," and is addressed as "Major" by
Esther's father. He is shown as a gentle, kindly old man with a
thick German accent. The man Esther has in mind was Washington Augustus Roebling, who directed construction of the Brooklyn Bridge, which was designed by his famous father, John A.
Roebling. Washington Roebling may have had a German accent
though he was born in Saxonburg, Pennsylvania. He served in the
Union Army during the Civil War and rose to the rank of colonel.
After the death of his father in 1869, he succeeded him and
supervised the construction which was completed in 1883. In this
partial portrait of the builder the implication is that the Brooklyn
Bridge is a triumph of German engineering. The designer was
indeed German born and was trained at the Royal Polytechnic
School in Berlin, but his son—who found it necessary to alter his
father's designs—was trained at Rensselaer Polytechnic Institute.
Wolfe, however, who was aware of the full truth, did not correct
Esther's impressions but he leaves the Brooklyn Bridge as a monument to German skill.

Wolfe's use of the title "Major" for the builder of the Brooklyn
Bridge is an interesting example of the fusion of his own memories with Esther's reminiscences. While Esther's father may have
addressed Colonel Roebling by his military rank, the title
"Major" probably came from another source. Major William
Cain was head of the Mathematics Department at the University
of North Carolina from 1889 until his retirement in 1920, the
year Thomas Wolfe was graduated. A noted engineer and mathe-
matician, Major Cain contributed to construction of the water

works system of New York City, the Pennsylvania Railroad, and the arches of the Brooklyn Bridge. The fact that Major Cain had played a part in the erection of Brooklyn Bridge was well known to the university students and was a source of local pride. When Wolfe wrote the account of the builder of the bridge he evidently drew on his Chapel Hill memories and transferred Major Cain's title to Washington Roebling.[15]

Consummate skill of a different kind is represented by Richard Brandell. Esther considers him the greatest actor she ever saw and, taking into account her wide theatrical experience, this opinion is high praise indeed. Yet with all his enormous talent combined with great personal charm and magnetism he nevertheless is a tormented man who feels that the world is conspiring against him; and he possesses an ineradicable taint, "the charlatanism and cheapness" with which the theater "corrupts its people." He has achieved the pinnacle of his profession but it brings him only nervous collapse after his magnificent performance in *Richard III*. Unlike Wolfe's other German characters he attempts to disguise his German heritage: "Although he insisted he was English by birth, he had been born in Leipzig, his father was a German; his real name was Brandl, which he had changed to Brandell after becoming an actor." This deception plus the "taint" of the theater result in a tragic flaw which Wolfe notes in a sweeping generalization: "Like most men who are conscious of something false and corrupt in them, he had a kind of Byronic scorn and self-contempt." In Wolfe's view any denial of national origin is odious.

The portrait of Brandell is modeled on Richard Mansfield, to whom Wolfe earlier refers by his real name. Mansfield was born in Berlin, the son of an English father and a German mother. Although he came to Boston with his mother in 1872, he returned to England in 1877 and became a polished actor. Later he achieved great fame in America, and Mrs. Bernstein's father was a member of Mansfield's troupe. Since Mansfield died in 1907, Wolfe never knew him and drew heavily on Mrs. Bernstein's memories. The resultant portrait of Mansfield as Brandell illustrates several of Wolfe's favorite ideas, but it is pertinent to this discussion only to note Wolfe's condemnation of the denial of national origin, which in this case is much more restrained than his denunciation of Abe Jones's denial of his Jewish origin.

Esther's cook, who is seen only in brief glimpses of *You Can't Go Home Again*, is not distinguished by a name but is referred to only as "Cook" or "Cookie." Cookie is portrayed as a dim-witted person possessing but one talent, her culinary skill. Esther says of her: "Well, she can cook, but after that she doesn't know April from July. And if you try to tell her anything she gets flustered and begins to gargle German at you." The Germanic passion for cleanliness and order is seen even in this stupid person; she keeps the kitchen immaculate. Her portrait is probably included to round out the full complement of Esther's servants rather realistically, but in it Wolfe includes traits he considered typical of the Germanic character: stupidity, skill, and love of order and cleanliness.

The love of order and cleanliness is also prominent in one of Wolfe's characters of German extraction, Otto Hauser, a manuscript reader for James Rodney & Co. Hauser would not have cleaning-women keep his apartment because "They were not clean and tidy enough to suit him." In Hauser's case this passion for order forces him to unusual behavior. As a publisher's reader he received many books but he would not keep them: "he gave his books away as soon as he finished reading them because he hated clutter, and books made clutter." Hauser also demonstrates his Germanic spirit in possessing a great skill, the uncanny ability to evaluate manuscripts.

This portrayal of Otto Hauser is taken from a short story, "No More Rivers," which Wolfe wrote in 1936. Perkins objected to it at that time because of the treatment of the publishing house of Scribner's, and the bulk of it remains unpublished. Aswell, however, did use a little of this material in Chapter 2 of *You Can't Go Home Again*. In the unpublished portion Wolfe clearly indicates that he considers Hauser (whom he calls George Hauser in the manuscript) an American.

> George [Hauser] was an American. We shall not pause here to tell you what that is:—we shall only say that George was an American the way a nigger is an American, the way a mountaineer down South is an American, the way a Vermonter in a valley [sic] is an American, the way a "tough mug" in the Cities is American, the way the Pennsylvania Dutchmen are Americans, the way the people with thin mouths, dry necks, hanks of hair, and all gnarled, seamed, *sweltered* out of them in Kansas, Iowa, and Illinois are Americans. George, in his own way, like all of them was an American. He came from German stock who had been in this country for a hundred years, and who were the first stock on earth —with all the fine intelligence, the sense of order and of balance, the warmth, the humanity, the tenderness, the exquisite sensitivity of the finest German stock, and with none of its brutality; nevertheless, George was American.[16]

The general impression of the German which Wolfe gives is on the whole a favorable one, but the German is not flawless. Germans achieve a high degree of acculturation, make solid citizens, and contribute desirable traits to the American character. It is significant that the post-Altamont Germans all possess a valuable skill: engineering, acting, culinary, or critical. But Otto Krause, Margaret Lutz, and Cookie exhibit a stupidity, a wooden insensitivity, which Wolfe also considered a facet of the German personality.

The readiness of Wolfe to admire Germanic qualities does not extend to the Dutch. Though immigrant Dutch characters are lacking in his published works, he manages to convey this impression by his treatment of persons of Dutch extraction. The Vanderbilts of course are of Dutch extraction but Wolfe did not think of them as Dutch. Like the other Ashevillians he was so awed by Vanderbilt wealth that they always symbolized the "filthy rich" to him. In writing of the Vanderbilts he uses two names: one is a crude disguise, Goulderbilt, effected by merging another symbol of robber-baron wealth, Gould, with the final syllables of Vanderbilt, which retains the Dutch flavor; the other name which Wolfe uses for Vanderbilt is Willets, an indication that the national origin of the family was not in his mind when he wrote about them. This was not the case, however, in his treatment of Carl Van Vechten. Van Vechten was actually a Midwesterner, a native of Iowa and a graduate of the University of Chicago, but his name is Dutch. Wolfe met Van Vechten in New York and strongly disliked him and all he stood for; Wolfe's contemptuous term for literary cults and fads was "Van Vechtenism." [17] Therefore, when he pillories Van Vechten in *The Web and the Rock* he dubs him "Van Vleeck, the novelist." Van Vleeck is not labeled as Dutch, but his name is as unmistakably so as is that of his prototype. But Wolfe's disapproval of the Dutch is not so much a blanket condemnation of all Dutch-Americans for his chief target is more localized, "the Hudson River Dutch" whom he satirizes in the person of Oswald Ten Eyck.

Ten Eyck is a student in the playwriting course at Harvard with Eugene Gant and is depicted as a miserable failure—both as a dramatist and as a man. Formerly an affluent journalist with the Hearst Syndicate, he is now so impoverished that he is forced to live in the cramped attic of an Irish family and to forego many of his meals to make ends meet. Ten Eyck's play is entitled "Dutch Fugue" and he purports to deal with "the quaintly flavored life and customs of his own people, the Hudson River Dutch." But the play should have been called "No Return," says Wolfe, because "brain bowed to belly" and the hungry dramatist could write only of food. It would be ironic indeed for Wolfe to condemn anyone for writing about food, and Eugene does not join in the scorn which the other members of the class heap upon Ten Eyck. What Wolfe objects to is Ten Eyck's inordinate pride of ancestry and his contempt for the Pennsylvania Dutch: "The little man was hotly proud of his ancestry and always insisted with a slight sneer of aristocratic contempt: 'Not the Pennsylvania Dutch—Good God, no! *They're* not Dutch but German: the *real* Dutch, the *old* Dutch, *Catskill* Dutch!'" After the failure of his play in Professor Hatcher's class, Ten Eyck proceeds to get drunk at one of Miss Potter's literary soirées and further disgrace himself by crude and irresponsible behavior. This event completes his utter ruin and he disappears by returning to New York. Thus one of the most resounding failures in all of Wolfe's books is made by the proud scion of "the Dutch, the Dutch, the *Catskill* Dutch."

Scandinavians are even fewer: there are no Danes at all; none of the eleven Swedish-born Ashevillians got into his books and the two Swedes from elsewhere that he depicts receive only the barest mention; and the sole Norwegian is only half-Norwegian at that. Wolfe was not oblivious to the Scandinavian element in America, for in a transcontinental sweep he does include it. Among the women of America he mentions in his paean in the "Young Faustus" section of *Of Time and the River* are those with typically Scandinavian names: "there are also immense and lovely girls, with a grip of a passionate bear, who have such names as Neilson, Lundquist, Jorgenson, and Brandt." However conscious he may have been of the Scandinavians in fancy, in fiction he almost ignores them.

The lone Norwegian is John Enborg, the service elevator operator in the Jacks' apartment building who loses his life in the fire which interrupts Mrs. Jack's party. Enborg is the faithful employee who respects the privileged class for whom he works and defends it against Henry, the embittered doorman, who is resentful of the wealthy and leisure class. Wolfe's narrative purpose in personalizing Enborg is partly to make the reader more sympathetic to his needless death and partly to show ramifications which underlie the rising class struggle in America (an aspect of Wolfe's social concern which lies beyond the scope of this study). Enborg is portrayed as half Norwegian and, surprisingly, as half Irish, but he betrays the national traits of neither, for he is represented as being typically American and therefore is symbolic of heteroge-

neous America which is distinctly different from the old world
stocks which are fused to produce the new. Enborg is thus different from most first-generation Americans whom Wolfe presents in
that all trace of the European origins of his parents has been
eradicated in him.

> John Enborg had been born in Brooklyn more than sixty years
> before, the son of a Norwegian seaman and an Irish serving-girl.
> In spite of his mixed parentage, one would have said without hesi-
> tation that he was "old stock" American—New England Yankee,
> most likely. Even his physical structure had taken on those na-
> tional characteristics which are perhaps the result, partly of
> weather and geography, partly of tempo, speech, and local custom
> —a special pattern of the nerves and vital energies wrought out
> upon the whole framework of flesh and bone, so that, from what-
> ever complex source they are derived, they are recognized in-
> stantly and unmistakably as "American." [18]

Although Enborg bears a Norwegian name, Wolfe presents him
not as Scandinavian but as a representative American. It is significant, though, that Wolfe selected a Norwegian-Irish combination
to produce a man who can be mistaken for "old stock" American.
Such a person would have to be of Northern European blood.

The treatment of the Scandinavians by Wolfe is more qualita-
tive than quantitative. He is cognizant of their presence and
considers Scandinavians as possessing the capability for complete
Americanization as evidenced in his choice of the paternity of
Enborg.[19] This implicit approval is the more emphatic since it
comes in Wolfe's late writing (1937), a time when he was more
careful and less impulsive in choosing his symbols.

Wolfe's only portrait of a gentile Polish-American is that of
Johnnie Adamowski, one of George Webber's chance traveling
companions who shares the experiences related in "I Have a
Thing to Tell You." Adamowski was born in Poland and emi-
grated to America at fifteen, where he is now a successful member
of a Wall Street firm and is a friend of Foxhall Edwards. Adamowski is "passionately American" and thoroughly devoted to his
adopted country, but his affection for America is not the materi-
alistic gratification which a European peasant finds in economic
fulfillment; Wolfe makes it clear that Adamowski came from the
Polish aristocracy. He is sick of Europe and eager to get back to
America, which he idealizes as the place "where all is peace and
freedom—where all is friendship—where all is love." Webber
considers this extravagant and intemperate language but he

shares Adamowski's point of view, and the resultant portrait reflects Wolfe's approval of this completely Americanized Polish aristocrat.

The Polish gentleman rounds out Wolfe's treatment of Americans from Northern Europe. In addition to the Welsh and Danes he does not include any Belgians, Finns, Baltics, or Russians. Omission of the Russians is somewhat surprising inasmuch as he had opportunity to know Russians in his youth. The seventy-two Russians who lived in Asheville constituted the second largest foreign-born contingent in the city, only five less than the English. Of the eight nationalities which he does include, however, he finds the Scotch most praiseworthy and the Irish the least, but his overall treatment of the Northern Europeans is favorable. It was Northern Europe which supplied the "old stock" Americans, and therefore put its stamp indelibly on the emergent American character. Therefore, since later immigrants from the same countries already possess the backgrounds which produced America in the first place, they are more rapidly assimilated than those from more divergent heritages. Thus the "new" Americans from Northern Europe are preferable to immigrants from elsewhere. "Blood will tell" is a cliché which Wolfe does not use, but in the America which he portrays, the best blood both originally and latterly came from Northern Europe.

Swart Strangers from Southern Europe

Wolfe's picture of Americans from Southern Europe is quite different. Lacking the blood and cultural ties which bound him to Northern Europe, he viewed the Southern Europeans as an altogether different breed. He was fully aware of their presence but mostly they are "dark-faced, dark-eyed, strange-tongued people" who constitute a large part of the "manswarm" on the streets of America's great urban centers. From these hordes he selects fewer characters than he does from Northern Europeans; there are no Spaniards, Portuguese, Hungarians, Yugoslavians, Rumanians, Bulgarians, or Albanians, but the other countries of Southern Europe are represented.

The French are almost non-existent; none of the dozen French-born Ashevillians is depicted, and Eugene Gant's first published encounter with the French comes when he sees French sailors swimming in the nude near their ship at Norfolk: "They came from France, he thought, and it is strange that they should be here." This impression was evidently a lasting one, for Wolfe portrays only one Frenchman in all the American settings of his books, an unnamed chauffeur in a vignette of the street. The "plump Frenchman with a waxed mustache, whose sentiments were decidedly revolutionary" is arguing politics and international economics and defending Russia to other chauffeurs. The Frenchman, who is depicted with the comic pomposity of a bantam rooster, displays Gallic volubility as he dances frenzily about the sidewalk gesticulating wildly. Becoming furious when his arguments are met with scorn, he lapses into elemental French. A "corky little American with cynical weariness" addresses him as "Frenchy" and rebuffs all his arguments. At this point George Webber walks away, leaving the Frenchman to bluster away at his unsympathetic hearers. Webber's sentiment is apparently the same as Eugene Gant's when he saw the nude swimmers. This brief portrait of the frustrated chauffeur is all Wolfe says of the French in America and when compared to his German portraits, for example, is very revealing. Wolfe once wrote: 'The French have always been to me the most *foreign* men in the world: I constantly get the sensation that they are creatures from another planet: I have never felt this with the English, Germans, or Austrians." His dislike of the European French was quite strong and is evident in the single portrait he gives of a French-American.

The Swiss, too, are represented by only a single portrait: "a burly devoted Swiss named Jannadeau, a grimy jeweller who rented a small fenced space among Gant's tombstones." Although Jannadeau appears a dozen times in *Look Homeward, Angel* and several times in *Of Time and the River,* he is a background figure whose chief trait is his loyalty to W. O. Gant—drunk or sober. Jannadeau is a slow-witted man of ponderous integrity, utterly lacking in any semblance of social grace, and whose fingers are habitually dirty. His one achievement (other than his occupation, the traditional Swiss trade of "watchmaker") is that he is assistant chief of the volunteer Altamont Fire Department. His portrait is not that of a prepossessing person; in fact, there is something pathetic about the patient Jannadeau.

Italians are more numerous for the simple reason that Wolfe encountered more Italians, and they appear in all his books. In Chapter XIV of *Look Homeward, Angel* in the panoramic awakening of Altamont, Wolfe pictures Pete Mascari opening his "fruit shop" for the day. With sensuous description he devotes a paragraph to the fruit shop but disposes of its proprietor in a single loaded sentence: "Light fell a moment on the ashen corpsiness of his face and on the liquid Sicilian poison of his eyes." The allusions to corpse, Sicily, and poison evoke the image of the treacherous Mafia in the mind of the reader and brand the fruit dealer as a sinister and unwelcome citizen.

This brief portrait appears to be that of the stereotyped Italian, but it too is drawn on a live model, and in this case Wolfe did not even bother to change the last name; only the first name is different. Charlie Mascari was an Asheville fruit dealer. However, the fact that he approximates the stereotype may be the reason that he was selected as the only one of the dozen native-born Italians for inclusion in *Look Homeward, Angel*. Wolfe's characters are usually too fully individualized to be considered mere stereotypes, but since some of them fit the stereotype pattern it may be that the existence of the stereotype in Wolfe's mind dictated the choice of the character as fictive material.

When Wolfe shifts his setting away from Asheville the Italians become more numerous, but the fullest discussion Wolfe gives of an Italian is his portrait of Guiseppe Pocallipo, the proprietor of the Italian speakeasy on West 46th Street where George Webber takes Esther to celebrate his twenty-fifth birthday. Pocallipo, known as Joe, had come to New York from a small village near Turin, and is essentially a decent and likable man who slipped into crime somewhat reluctantly. In the beginning Joe and his wife were hardworking, law-abiding immigrants seeking to earn their own way in their new country; he was a waiter in a large hotel and she operated a rented rooming house. She began to serve meals and Joe helped her on week-ends. The diners wanted wine with their meals, despite the fact that the Prohibition Act had taken effect, and to an Italian this seemed completely reasonable. Joe found that wine was available and the profits from it were large. This discovery led him into the operation of a speakeasy which brought him rapid wealth.

Wolfe stresses the fact that Joe faced a moral choice between two difficult alternatives. He could remain honest and decent and continue as a waiter but this would lead only to old age, poverty and broken feet. On the other hand, operation of a speakeasy would lead him "if not into full membership in the criminal underworld, at least into collusion with it; into a bought-and-paid-for treaty with the criminal police; and to violence, dishonesty, and crime," but the financial rewards were huge. Wolfe says of Joe that "like many another simple man of the corrupted period, it seemed to him there was no choice to make."

The real villain according to Wolfe is Prohibition, and Joe is pictured as more of a victim than villain; his portrait is actually a rather sympathetic one. But Joe does allow himself to be victimized and does drift into crime. Wolfe does not say that Italians are more prone to crime than Northern Europeans, and it is highly likely that the operator of the speakeasy Wolfe visited was an Italian. Nevertheless, Wolfe was describing the lawless twenties and the preponderance of Italian names among the best known criminals of that era could hardly have failed to make an impression. It is therefore significant that Wolfe's one depiction of an immigrant's step-by-step descent into crime is not a sturdy Scot or a stalwart German but an Italian. No other Italian portrayal approaches Joe Pocallipo in detail, though Wolfe mentions other Italians from time to time.

Slavs are another group little noted by Wolfe. Russians, of course, are one of his most notable omissions, but he hardly mentions the South Slavs either. In describing the lobby scenes of the Hotel Leopold he notes: "Over behind the cigar counter, the vender, a fat Czechish youth with a pale flabby face and dull taffy-colored hair, was industriously engaged in picking his fat nose with a greasy thumb and forefinger." This portrait is unflattering enough, but Wolfe is no more complimentary when he describes a group of Slavs. In "Death the Proud Brother" two Slavic couples are among the viewers of the fourth death, and Wolfe categorizes the four with sharp criticism.

> They all had the thick clumsy fingers, the dull-red smouldering complexions, the taffy-colored hair, bleared eyes, and broad, blunted, smeared features of the Slavic races—of Lithuanians or Czechs—and for a while they stared stupidly and brutally at the figure of the dead man, and then began to talk rapidly among themselves in coarse thick tones, and a strange tongue.[20]

In displaying this attitude toward the Slavs, Wolfe shows that he considered them no asset to America, and it is no wonder that he is not further concerned with the Slavic element in the melting pot.

The Greeks also constitute an inferior species of Americans, though they are much more numerous. In presenting the Greeks, Wolfe relies heavily on the stereotype, for his Greeks are almost invariably "lunch-room Greeks." Like most people who have received a classical education, Wolfe had a profound admiration for the cultural heritage of ancient Greece, but of all the Greeks he depicts not one seems to be aware of the glory that was Greece.

In the "Kronos and Rhea: The Dream of Time" section in *Of Time and the River* he equates the Greeks and railway lunch counters.

> Delicately they dive for Greeks before the railway station: the canoe glides gently through the portals of the waiting room (for whites). Full fathom five the carcass of old man Lype is lying (of his bones is coral made) and delicately they dive for lunch-room Greeks before the railway station.

This interesting paragraph reveals several features of Wolfe's creative technique: his indebtedness to Joyce's *Ulysses,* his delight in parody, his fondness for literary quotation, and his use of memory. But the net result of his adaptation of the widely used Drowned Man *motif* is a reflection of his prejudice which produces another instance of the Greek stereotype. While the entire Kronos and Rhea section is obviously Joycean in execution, this passage is an immediate parallel to that of Stephen Dedalus's thoughts about a drowned man in the "Proteus" episode of *Ulysses*. Wolfe's target for parody is a favorite one, T. S. Eliot; in this paragraph he parodies Parts I and IV of *The Waste Land*. And, like both Joyce and Eliot in these instances, he draws upon Shakespeare for well-turned phrases in using two lines of Ariel's song in *The Tempest*. But in the selection of the drowned man he relies, characteristically, on his own memory and chooses an Asheville man.

One of the most spectacular events Wolfe witnessed in his youth was the great flood of July 1916, perhaps the worst that Western North Carolina ever experienced. The French Broad River rose disastrously, isolated Asheville, and inundated the suburb of Biltmore, taking several lives. Wolfe refers to this flood a number of times in his writing. Earlier in *Of Time and the River* he mentions "the two Lipe girls" and says, *"They lived in Biltburn by the river, and one of them was drowned in the flood."* While they were reported dead at the time, both Lipe girls survived the flood, and their father was drowned.[21] It is Mr. Lipe who became "old man Lype," the symbolic corpse. James Cornelius Lipe was captain of the Biltmore Fire Department and a foreman at the Biltmore Estate, but he was not Greek. There is no mention of a Greek name among the dead listed in the newspaper accounts of the 1916 flood. Thus when Wolfe employed a universal *motif* of abstract symbolism he fused with it the concrete image of an actual person from his own memory. He localized the setting in his mind (the Biltmore railroad station), thought of a specific drowned man (Mr. Lipe), and changed the nationality of the classic image from Phoenician to Greek. Then, in attempting to universalize his fused image, he reverts to his stereotype and the drowned men, instead of being abstract symbols of death, become merely dead "lunch-room Greeks."

Wolfe pictures the Greeks in various lights, all of them unflattering. To one he gives the infallible Wolfean sign of low intelligence, a narrow brow. When Eugene watches a man in upstate New York pick up a prostitute, Wolfe says of him, "he looked like a prosperous Greek; he had a strong, swarthy, brutal face, full of sensual assurance." In discussing the Saturday night habits of Americans, he says that they go to "saloons along Third Avenue or the Greek's place in a little town" but in either case the results are the same: "hard whiskey, gin, and drunkenness, and brawls and fights and vomit." The Greeks in Wolfe's panorama are far removed indeed from those who wrote the *Iliad*, the *Republic*, and *Oedipus Rex,* who carved the Venus de Milo, and who built the Parthenon. The *raison d'être* of the Greeks in America, according to Wolfe's portrayal, is to operate unsavory lunchrooms.

The overall presentation of the Southern Europeans reveals a lack of tolerance for them. The eight nationalities of Northern Europe which he portrays have contributed the strength and stability of the American nation; in sharp contrast, the five nationalities of Southern Europe are distinctly inferior and have contributed nothing. Wolfe's dislike for Gallic ways is seen in the left-wing French chauffeur who is attempting to foment trouble and arouse disloyalty, and the sole Swiss has rugged integrity and dogged loyalty but still he picks his nose with dirty fingers. The Italians, for all their likable qualities of warmth and gusto, are still sinister and prone to crime, and the Czechs are dismissed as hopeless louts. The Olympian grandeur of the Greeks, like Sappho's songs, vanished long before the modern Greeks arrived in America. Though sometimes muscular, their strength does not till the soil or drive machines; their mission is to operate greasy lunchrooms and serve unpalatable food to the "real" Americans. In his depiction of the Southern Europeans Wolfe makes more use of stereotyped characters than he does in portraying Northern Europeans. The Swiss and the Italians both approximate the common stereotypes, and the picture of the Czech plays upon the Slavic stereotype. But in the case of the Greeks he employs the stereotype with a rigidity and consistency that is unusual in his writing. In "Death the Proud Brother" he contrasts Northern and Southern Europeans as he observed them on New York's upper East Side.

> These streets were seething with the violent and disorderly life of dark-faced, dark-eyed, strange-tongued people, who surged back and forth, innumerably, namelessly, with the tidal, liquid, and swarming fluency that all dark bloods and races have, so that the lean precision, the isolation, and the severe design characteristic of the lives of northern peoples—like something lonely, small, pitifully yet grandly itself—are fractured instantly by this tidal darkness. The numberless and ageless manswarm of the earth is instantly revealed in all its fathomless horror, and will haunt one later in dreams, even if one sees only a half-dozen of these dark faces in a street.[22]

Travelers from Antique Lands

While Wolfe centers his interest upon Europeans, he does portray some Asiatics. Characters from the Middle East are not only infrequent but receive scant attention. Natives of the Middle East were understandably few in Asheville and none of the three Turks is pictured in *Look Homeward, Angel,* nor are Turks portrayed elsewhere in Wolfe's fiction. The only representative of the Middle East in *Look Homeward, Angel* is a Persian who is seen in a brief glimpse. As Eugene Gant and George Graves take their walk through the town one of the people they meet is Mr. Buse, the oriental rug merchant, but all Wolfe has to say of him is that "His broad dark face was wreathed in Persian smiles." Since Mr. Buse does not appear again in Wolfe's books, nor do any other Persians, the impact of Iran is confined to one broad smile.

The change of setting to New York does not increase the number of Middle Easterners in Wolfe's kaleidoscopic fiction. In *The Story of a Novel* he says that after his return to America in 1931 he moved into a little basement flat "in the Assyrian quarter of South Brooklyn," but none of his Assyrian neighbors found a place in his fiction. In his satiric essay "On Leprechauns," Wolfe uses as his introduction some remarks that he attributes to "An Armenian friend of ours, a Mr. Vladimir Adzigian of South Brooklyn," but aside from the purported remarks, he makes no other mention of Mr. Adzigian and proceeds to make a stinging attack on the Irish. In Chapter 27 of *You Can't Go Home Again* entitled "The Locusts Have No King" Wolfe treats "the huge and rusty jungle of South Brooklyn" as a cosmos. Among George Webber's experiences there is an incident when a waiter tries to give George the plot for a story, an Armenian story, but the story bores George immeasurably. Apparently the Armenians did too. There was a large Armenian colony on Atlantic Avenue, near where Wolfe lived, but except for the brief references to Mr. Adzigian no Armenians appear in Wolfe's writing. He took cognizance of the fact that immigrants came from the Middle East, but for them the usually voluble Wolfe has hardly a word. They are merely travelers from an antique land.

Inscrutable Orientals

Wolfe shows more interest in the characters from the Far East and their portraits are fuller. Though he includes Chinese and Japanese, both members of the yellow race, he designates them by nationality and emphasizes their distinctive qualities rather than their racial commonalty. It is apparent that he thought of them as widely differing nationalities, and in the treatment of his Oriental characters he invariably labels them by country and not by race.

Of the two groups the Chinese are the more frequent in his writing. Part of Wolfe's purpose in the inclusion of Chinese, especially in "The Web of Earth," is the characterization of W. O. Gant. To old Gant all Chinamen were Ah Sins, and he had an abiding and violent hatred for them. Eliza felt that his hatred must have some basis in fact, some grievance perhaps, but Gant denied it. At the time of the Boxer Rebellion Gant was elated and was eager to join the fray: "They've declared war on China, and I'm going to enlist, by God, I will!" One of Wolfe's fine comic scenes occurs when Gant attempts to retrieve his shirts from a Chinese laundry without his ticket. Wolfe depicts the two Chinese laundrymen as typical stereotypes confronted by the irate Gant, who is roaring drunk. Gant's attitude is typical of the anti-Chinese feeling of his time and his distrust of them is shared to some extent by Eliza. She remarks of the laundrymen: "There was a look in the eyes of those men I didn't like; it made my flesh crawl!" A similar opinion is also held by her brother Bascom who delivers a vigorous denunciation of Chinese laundrymen in *Of Time and the River*.

Gant's hatred for the Chinese also affords Wolfe another comic scene. Gant frequently patronized Ambrose Radiker's saloon which employed a mulatto, "big yellow nigger Dan." On one occasion when Gant was drunk he decided Dan was a Chinaman and endeavored to kill him, frightening the hapless Dan almost out of his wits. Wolfe neither apologizes for nor attempts to explain W. O. Gant's inchoate hatred of the Chinese. Although he depicts it as comic exaggeration in Gant's case, the instinctive American dislike for the Chinese was too common an attitude to warrant comment, especially concerning a person who had witnessed the violent extremes to which anti-Chinese agitation went in the 1870's and 1880's as Gant had.

Unlike W. O. Gant, Jerry Alsop is portrayed as being attracted by the Chinese. Alsop is pictured as having the true provincial's zest to discover the strange and unusual in New York and this led him to the unknown edibles of Chinatown which resulted in a strange fascination: "He had a love for Chinatown, chop suey, and the pungent sauce: it was abundant, it was cheap. The strange faces of the Chinks, the moisty vapors, Oriental and somewhat depressant, all delighted him." Wolfe expresses contempt for such an attitude with the withering line: "His taste, like Dr. Samuel Johnson's, was not fine—he liked abundance and he liked to slop in it."

Wolfe's main portrait of a Chinese is Mr. Wang, who lives at the Murphys' and like Eugene is a student at Harvard. His rooms are furnished in oriental luxury and the odor of incense is heavy. Wang is jovial and friendly but Eugene discovers Wang is also stupid and lazy when he tries to help Wang with his English compositions. Wang likes to joke with Eugene and takes him to expensive Chinese restaurants and showers gifts upon him, for money is no item with Wang. Wolfe sums Wang up as "just a fat, stupid, indolent, and good-hearted child," but he is also kind and proves himself a friend in need. Late one night Eugene received a telegram that his father was dying and Wang lent him fifty dollars to make the trip home and presented him with "two magnificent fans of peacock feathers." Herein is another of Wolfe's splendid ironies; when W. O. Gant, the great Chinese hater, is dying, it is a Chinese who advances the money for Eugene to go to his father's bedside.

Wolfe's total picture of the Chinese is an unfavorable one. He accepted the prevailing Chinese stereotype and, unlike Mark Twain in *Roughing It*, he nowhere defends the Chinese. He employs them as comic figures and laughs at them rather than with them. The Chinese stand in Wolfe's fiction as symbols of the strange and the ludicrous. The Chinese are not only unassimilated but are unassimilatable, and therefore remain forever alien and perennially humorous.

While Wolfe rarely has a Japanese as a background figure, such as the anonymous Japanese lover of the profligate heiress, Amy Carleton, he does give a rather full portrait of a Japanese sculptor in "The Microscopic Gentleman from Japan." The sculptor occupies the apartment under George Webber's and is annoyed by Webber's pacing the floor late at night. But Katamoto makes a huge joke of the matter and wins George's friendship and admiration by his unfailing good-nature and courtesy.

Katamoto's rooms are also furnished from his homeland and like Wang's there is a strong smell of incense, but unlike Wang's ornate and bizarre luxury, Katamoto's furnishings are graceful and delicate. The rooms also include Katamoto's studio where he fashioned enormous statues of politicians, an art "he had mastered with true Japanese fidelity," and unlike the lazy Wang, he was a dynamo of energy. After finishing a statue, Katamoto would, says Wolfe, lifting a phrase from Whitman, "loaf and invite his soul."

Wolfe uses some aspects of the Japanese stereotype in the characterizations of Katamoto, such as his ingratiating smile, his patient courtesy, and his quick adaptation to profit in his work from American taste in sculpture. But Katamoto is more fully portrayed than Wang and the Japanese's childlike humor appeals to Wolfe and he laughs *with* him rather than at him, as he does at the Chinese. Katamoto's portrait is a favorable one and reflects the respect of the writer for the artist. When Katamoto dies, George is informed of his death by another Japanese "with a toothy grin of frozen courtesy." Though George sensed the Orient more strongly in this man, it is quite apparent from Wolfe's portraits of the Orientals that he preferred the Japanese to the Chinese.

This preference for the Japanese over the Chinese reflects the general attitude of most Americans during the first quarter of the twentieth century. The general antagonism toward the Chinese during the late nineteenth century was reinforced by the Boxer Rebellion, which further aroused America's dislike for the Chinese. In contrast to this feeling was the friendliness most Americans displayed for the Japanese after the country was opened to the West by Commodore Perry. Japan emulated American technology, always flattering to the originator, and was generally regarded as the most progressive country in the Orient. This good will was further enhanced by Japan's participation in World

War I on the side of the Allies, and it was not until the Japanese invasion of Manchuria in 1931 that American feeling for Japan began to shift. Wolfe's depiction of the Japanese as preferable to the Chinese is but another instance in which his writing displays the milieu in which he grew up and attained manhood.

In spite of Wolfe's keen sensitivity for national origin and his avowed purpose, his presentation of the foreigner is haphazard and unsystematic. When Joel Pierce's proud, patrician mother asked Eugene Gant what he found on his nocturnal prowls of New York's East Side, he answered "People." But to her inquiry of what kind of people he can only stammer "all kinds." However, unlike his *alter ego,* when the fluent Wolfe took pencil in hand he recorded his impressions and indicated his awareness of the polyglot composition of America's greatest city with a Whitmanesque catalogue.

> The mongrel compost of a hundred races—the Jews, the Irish, the Italians, and the niggers, the Swedes, the Germans, the Lithuanians and the Poles, the Russians, Czechs, and Greeks, the Syrians, Turks and Armenians, the nameless hodge-podge of the Balkans, as well as Chinese, Japs, and dapper little Filipinos—a hundred tongues, a thousand tribes . . . all poured in through the lean gateways of the sea . . . all wrought and woven . . . into the great web of America. . . .[23]

Hence the East Side was a microcosm containing the ingredients, still raw and unassimilated, that had gone into the melting pot to produce the phenomenon that is America. But Wolfe was not a sociologist and, in spite of his fascination with the East Side, he did not turn to it as a scientist might for laboratory material. Instead he drew his fictive material from his own background and experience, which was sufficiently wide for him to include the twenty nationalities which he presents. Through these portraits, some of which are quite ancillary to his narrative purpose, he emphasizes the diverse composition of America and gives his assessment of the component elements. It was Wolfe's intent to weave into the fabric of his fiction "the great web of America," and his treatment of the foreigner is thus representative of the multiformity of America and therefore artistically sound.

Wolfe's portraits are not the only means he employs to portray America as a melting pot of the earth, as his Whitmanesque catalogues also seek the same purpose, but the catalogues are less effective, even when they are set in the frame of conscious symbolism. For example, the apartment house fire in which John Enborg perishes is symbolic of the conglomerate nature of America: "a mixture of a dozen races and their excited babel of strange tongues. There were German cooks, and French maids, English butlers and Irish serving girls. There were Swedes and Danes and Italians and Norwegians, with a sprinkling of White Russians. There were Poles and Czechs and Austrians, Negroes and Hungarians." And Wolfe's symbolic cipher, C. Green, is a composite of several national origins: "A little Scotch, perhaps, was Green, a little Irish, English, Spanish even, and some German—a little of each part, all compacted and exploded into nameless atom of America!" But his individualized portraits are certainly the most effective and dramatic presentation of what he wished to show about America.

Wolfe's standard for evaluating the foreigner is the nativistic touchstone of Americanization—the degree to which the foreigner is capable of complete acculturation. Thus the Oriental cannot be assimilated and is therefore undesirable except to add an exotic coloring that may be diverting at times, and for this purpose the Japanese are preferable to the Chinese. Wolfe is too vague on the Middle Easterners to draw a firm conclusion about them; though he seems to imply that while they are more acculturated than the Orientals, they are less so than the Europeans; at any rate his attitude toward them is one of patronizing toleration, just as it is toward Latin Americans. But in the case of the Europeans, he is much more explicit.

During the 1920's Madison Grant, more than anyone else, "taught the American people to recognize within the white race a three-tiered hierarchy of Mediterraneans, Alpines, and Nordics, to identify themselves as Nordic, and to regard any mixture with the other two as a destructive process of 'mongrelization.' " [24] It is not known whether Wolfe read Grant or not; he would not have had to, for Grant's ideas were very much in the air during the tribal twenties. Neither is it likely that Wolfe had to be taught to identify himself as Nordic. Although his Nordic self-identification is unwavering, he could on occasion satirize the idea of Nordic superiority as he did in his amusing sketch of the torture instruments in the Tower of London.

> It will no doubt be pleasing to all of us who are quite sure of the Nordic supremacy in all matters requiring character and courage and honesty, and who believe that only by the continued domination of the Nordic may civilization be saved, to know that in

the matter of devising abominable and revolting cruelties for the torture of the unconvinced we Nordics have shown the same superiority.[25]

But despite such occasional satiric thrusts, Wolfe's fictional assessment of the strength and stability of the composite American character traces their origins to Nordic sources.

His portraits of hyphenated Americans from Europe are of a two-tiered rather than three-tiered structure, but many express agreement with the Grant idea that the infusion of Southern European blood resulted in "mongrelization." Wolfe's favorite term for polyglot Americans that included Southern Europeans was "mongrel compost." As a young man during his first summer in New York he wrote his mother expressing his dismay at immigration from Southern Europe.

> Yet, yearly we are bringing hundreds of thousands of inferior people—the Latin races, undeveloped physically, dwarfed mentally, into this country. From them will grow the America of to-morrow —"the hope of the world." It is impossible to regard them without a sinking of the heart. How can anything good come from it? I am no pessimist, but why try to side-step the facts? [26]

Even his realization that the South was "for the most part of undiluted stock" brought him small comfort. Most of his fictional portraits do not indicate a major shift from the attitude expressed in 1923; the Northern Europeans reinforced the strength of the American character but the Southern Europeans were simply an unwelcome dilution which would be detrimental to American greatness.

The polarity of Wolfe's thinking which led him to use such characteristic terminology as "Jews, Gentiles, foreigners, and Americans" resulted in portrayal of non-native Americans with acute awareness of their national origin. Writing from the Anglo-Saxon, Protestant viewpoint of the "old" American, he regarded all newcomers as interlopers. Though he may euphemistically refer to them as "new" Americans, until they become fully acculturated they are still foreigners to Thomas Wolfe, and their acceptability is very definitely determined by national origin; and at the time he was writing, a majority of his countrymen would have agreed with him.

5 The Indian:

'The Honest Tang of America'

Some treatment of the Indian is to be expected in the work of any writer whose scope is as vast as Wolfe's. As a writer whose historical reach extended back to the primeval wilderness of America he was bound to include the Indian at some point in his writing. Also the fact that he drew so heavily on his own region, which was still inhabited by Indians in his own lifetime, made it almost inevitable that he would deal somewhere with the Indian. But compared to his numerous references to the Negro and his extensive portrayal of the Jew, the Indian is but sketchily drawn.

The Indians of Old Catawba

Wolfe turned to the Indian for his fictional name for North Carolina, Old Catawba,[1] and his fondness for Indian names caused him to include them in his rhapsodic catalogues. Though he has various incidental references and uses anecdotes about the Indians, the significance of the Indian does not lie in Wolfe's total picture of the red man, but rather two specific instances—one humorous, the other serious.

The humorous instance occurs in his unfinished historical novel, *The Hills Beyond*, where he recounts the original colonization of Old Catawba and gives his own version of the fate of the celebrated Lost Colony. Wolfe takes some artistic license: he juggles the historical facts and has the colony founded a decade later

than it actually was and by a different man. He does follow the
general tradition in maintaining that the inhabitants of the Lost
Colony intermarried with the Indians and left mixed-blood descendants, although his interest in the subject is by no means
comparable to the serious treatment that his one-time college
classmate, Paul Green, gave to it in *The Lost Colony.*

Wolfe uses these mixed-blood descendants of the Lost Colony as
an occasion to satirize the aristocratic pretensions of tidewater
North Carolina. He pictures the East as seizing on the idea of
half-breed descendants of the Lost Colony to provide itself with
an English ancestry antedating both Plymouth and Jamestown,
and from something which began merely as a titillating thought
there arose an unshakable conviction of descent from the pre-
sumptive survivors of the Lost Colony. The result of this fanciful
logic was the formation of still another organization whose requis-
ite for membership depended upon the time of ancestral residence
in America.

> In almost no time at all a new and highly exclusive social organ-
> ization came into being, calling itself The Society of the Sons and
> Daughters of the Aborigines. The aristocratic pretensions of its
> members threatened overnight to eclipse even the haughty claims
> of the F.F.V.'s and the Mayflower descendants. The Sons and
> Daughters of the Aborigines had just discovered who they were,
> and from this point on they would play second fiddle to no one.
> No doubt it was all well enough, they said patronizingly, to talk
> about royal grants and tide-water plantations and the early days of
> Plymouth, but such trifling originalities as these could not be ex-
> pected to matter very greatly to people who were *aboriginally* de-
> scended from the *first* English colonists *and* from Indian chief-
> tains. It was quite surprising to see how proudly the Aborigines
> laid claim to this tinge of savage color in their veins. Ladies whose
> husbands would have reached for their dueling pistols at any im-
> putation of a *recent* tinge of color in their blood felt no hesitation
> whatever in proclaiming their dusky ancestors of some two and a
> half centuries before.[2]

As comic satire this account ridicules all societies and groups
whose claims to aristocracy are dependent upon date of first residence in America, not only the examples Wolfe gives, F.F.V.'s
(First Families of Virginia) and Mayflower descendants, but
those unnamed, too, such as the Colonial Dames of America, the
Daughters of the American Revolution, the Society of the Cincin-
nati, and others. With tongue-in-check he points out that the
logical extent of such pretension would be to claim Indian de-

scent, as Will Rogers used to do in humorously asserting that his ancestors had not come on the Mayflower but had met the boat. But Wolfe also observes that among the aristocratically pretentious a "tinge of savage color"—even red—is acceptable only if it is remote. In laughing at the spurious "Society of the Sons and Daughters of the Aborigines" Wolfe not only betrays the tone of social criticism that becomes more definite in his later works but is also indulging the mountaineer's disdain for the pretentious airs of the tidewater.

The serious use of the Indian is found in his Indian characters, which are limited to three—all Cherokees and all of mixed blood. Asheville is located in what was once Cherokee domain, and during the removal of the Cherokees to Indian Territory in 1838–1839 a large number of them escaped and remained in the mountain fastness of North Carolina where their descendants are still living and are known as Eastern Cherokees. The Eastern Cherokees settled in the Great Smoky Mountains and live mainly in Swain, Jackson and Graham counties. These counties are west of Asheville (Swain and Graham join Tennessee) and although the distance is not great, in Wolfe's boyhood the communications with them were extremely poor and it is unlikely that he visited any of these Indian areas in his formative years. Though Indians did live in several other North Carolina counties, Buncombe was not one of them. The 1900 census does not report any Indians in Buncombe County, and the 1910 census reports only one. In the light of these figures it is not surprising that no full-blooded Indians turn up among the acquaintances of Eugene Gant and George Webber.

The only Indian character in the Gant cycle is Mrs. Morgan, one of the mysterious flotsam of boarders who touch Eugene's life only by a sudden and relatively short stay at Dixieland and then retire into the inglorious nullity from whence they came. Mrs. Morgan came from a mountain town in the western part of the state, had an illegitimate baby, and two weeks later vanished forever. The adolescent Eugene took in this little drama with wide-eyed wonder, accepting the birth of the baby with youthful romanticizing of both birth and the Indian blood, and Wolfe gives Eugene's thoughts in a Joycean stream-of-consciousness: "Deep womb, dark flower. The Hidden. The secret fruit, heart red, fed by rich Indian blood. Womb-night brooding darkness flowering secretly into life." Wolfe casts over her an aura of the mysterious that the romantic imagination associates with the Indian. While the Indian is also victim of human frailty, there is in him an occult racial amplitude that is somehow admirable even though unfathomable.

The Cranes of Libya Hill

This racial amplitude, which is only hinted at in the case of Mrs. Morgan, is developed more fully in Wolfe's other two Indian characters, Captain John Crane and his son Nebraska, both of whom appear in the Webber cycle. Wolfe intended the Cranes to be an entire family. In a sketch entitled "Characters: People of the Street" which he prepared in 1936 for "The Vision of Spangler's Paul," he projected his plans for five members to comprise the Crane family.

> *The Cranes*
> *Nebraska,* at the opening of the story, aged 14, and previously described, *John Crane, Nebraska's father,* a policeman, an ex-professional wrestler and occasionally still a participant in local exhibitions.
> *Little Buzz,* Nebraska's younger brother, at this time aged five, drinks beer and smokes cigars to the huge delight and pride of the rest of the family.
> *Nell,* Nebraska's sister, aged thirteen, already as large and as mature as a woman.
> *Mrs. Crane,* the daughter of a butcher, a giant of a woman, as brutal, as savage as unhalted nature, also as warm, as true, a natural force of a woman. This completes the Crane family.[3]

Of the five, however, only Captain Crane and Nebraska appeared in print. It is unfortunate that Wolfe was unable to complete this remarkable family which he was still developing at the time of his death. Little Buzz would certainly have made an interesting addition to the Wolfe gallery.

Captain Crane is part Cherokee, but Wolfe indicates it is not a very large part: "Nebraska's father had been a policeman, was now a captain on the force; he came from back in Zebulon County; he had some Cherokee in him." And having said that, Wolfe does not again overtly identify him as part Indian. In his physical description of Captain Crane Wolfe does not give him any features that would cause the reader to suspect the presence of Indian blood if he had not already mentioned it. Captain Crane's racial inheritance from the red man is indicated by traits of character rather than his physical appearance. Like his son Nebraska, he "seemed to have come straight from the heart of immutable and unperturbed nature."

In the characterization of Crane as wrestler, as well as policeman, Wolfe maintains his chief trait is absolute fearlessness. In keeping with Crane's earthy nature, Wolfe uses a series of homely nineteenth-century clichés to describe him in the ring: "Mr. Crane was as loose as ashes, as cold as a potato, patient as a dray-horse, and as excited as a bale of hay." In this trait of absolute fearlessness Wolfe suggests that Mr. Crane is not only a brave man in the tradition of a Rustam or a Sir Lancelot but rather that Crane's valor is the heritage of primitive ancestors, the fearlessness of Cooper's Uncas or Simms's Sanutee. This hint is more fully explicated in the characterization of his son Nebraska, for they are indeed an instance of like father, like son: "That man did not know what fear was—and his son was like him in all ways, and the best and bravest boy in town!"

Nebraska Crane is one of the most winsome characters Wolfe ever created, and one of the most important symbolically. As George Webber's childhood playmate, his boon companion in youth, and later as a star big-league baseball player he exemplifies some of the finest qualities of unspoiled youth and the realization of the American dream. In many ways he is as typically an American boy as Tom Sawyer and Penrod Schofield, but with the added dimension they would have achieved had they grown up to become a Ty Cobb or a Babe Ruth. Though he is an idealized character in some ways, he is in others real and vital, and Nebraska is the kind of person any boy would be proud to have as his friend. It is no wonder that Edward Aswell maintained that in "making him George Webber's best friend" Wolfe did so "because that was the kind of friend the youthful Tom Wolfe always wanted and never had." [4] But in drawing the lineaments of Nebraska, Wolfe achieved considerably more than wish fulfillment: he created an engaging and enduring character who, unlike the other major characters, obscured his prototype (or prototypes) for two decades, and who stands as an important symbol of Wolfe's basic ideas.

Nebraska differs from Tom Sawyer and Penrod in one important particular, however; he is even more "American" than they, for in his veins flows the rich red blood of the Cherokee. Wolfe stresses Nebraska's Indian blood almost as much as he emphasizes Abraham Jones's Jewish blood. In Nebraska's first appearance in *The Web and the Rock* there is a one-paragraph description of him which accentuates his Indian blood and is prophetic of his adult career.

Nebraska Crane was walking down the street upon the other side. He was bare-headed, his *shock of Indian coarse black hair* standing out, his shirt was opened at his strong, lean neck, his square *brown face* was tanned and flushed with recent effort. From the big pocket of his pants the thick black fingers of a fielder's mitt protruded, and upon his shoulder he was carrying a well-worn ash-wood bat . . . as he passed, he turned his *fearless face* upon the boy across the street—looked at him with his *black-eyed Indian look.*[5] (Italics mine.)

Wolfe is unusually persistent in referring to Nebraska's Indian blood. When Nebraska faces the four boys who were threatening Webber, he kept "his black Indian gaze fixed steadily upon them." Nebraska's response to the excitement engendered by Dick Prosser's wild behavior was that his "coal black eyes were shining. . . . The awakened blood of the Cherokee was smoking in him." When the adult Webber encounters Nebraska years later, the Indian is still accentuated. At their meeting on the train Nebraska's "tar-black Cherokee eyes looked out with the same straight deadly fearlessness." As they renewed their friendship "George saw that the Cherokee in him was the same now as it had been when he was a boy."

Wolfe could not have expressed any greater fondness for Nebraska than he did in making Nebraska a baseball player. When he wrote of the twelve-year-old Eugene Gant, "He played games badly, although he took a violent interest in sports," he expressed the literal truth on both counts. The gangling Wolfe was too lacking in muscular coordination to play any game well (except pitching horseshoes),[6] but he greatly admired athletes and his favorite sport, by all odds, was baseball. Wolfe not only loved the game itself (he delighted in watching it and even in listening to a game over the radio), but in his ceaseless search for symbols it seemed to him that his favorite sport best symbolized what is distinctly American—the humble America that he loved. He clearly expressed this meaning in a letter to Arthur Mann, the sports writer. In an unpublished holograph manuscript Wolfe traces the baseball career of Nebraska and makes him a major league star.

The life of Nebraska Drake [an earlier name for Crane] had been a happy one: he had played baseball, and he had been good at it. Nebraska had begun his career as a professional player in 1917 as a member of the Knoxville team in the South Atlantic league.[7] At that time he was only nineteen years old; he played in 124 games that year and hit for 356. In 1918, he was bought by the Birmingham team of the Southern association, played in every game, and hit for an average of 337 per cent. He was purchased by the New York American league team that year; and in 1919 played in 27 games for that team and hit for 284. In 1920, about a month after the beginning of the season, the centre-fielder of the Yankees broke a bone in his ankle; Nebraska played the remainder of the season and hit for [19, crossed out] 296. At this time he was twenty-two years old, and had already [three years, crossed out] four years playing experience in organized baseball. The following year, he was given the centre-fielder's position from the commencement of the season; he was twenty-two [three?] years old that year, and had the greatest year any young player in base ball had had since the emergence of Ty Cobb.

In that year, Drake hit for a percentage of 386, and led the league.[8] [breaks off]

But the waning career of Nebraska brings to Webber the sharp realization that professional athletics also are, in the words of Housman, "fields where glory does not stay." Wolfe had earlier treated the brevity of the glory of the amateur athlete in his portrait of Jim Randolph, the star halfback of Pine Rock College who afterwards in the stern competition of New York could not repeat the triumphs of his athletic feats. Though surrounded for a time by a little band of hero-worshipers, his fame faded and left him an embittered and maladjusted man. When Nebraska reveals his impending retirement from baseball, the thought comes to Webber: would good old Nebraska repeat the tragic pattern of Jim Randolph? What would be the effect on the simple Cherokee when he returned to the mountains?

Two of Wolfe's most compelling concerns in life were the quest "of that fair Medusa, Fame" and the passing of Time. In his later writing he sometimes combines these two fixations into a single interest—the effect of time on a person who has achieved fame. His most celebrated study is of course his penetrating analysis of Sinclair Lewis as Lloyd McHarg. And in the case of Nebraska Crane, Wolfe is concerned with the effect of fame on the man when he leaves the cheers of idolizing fans far behind him and returns to rural Zebulon. The grounds of his concern lie in the fact that athletic fame is achieved earlier in life than other kinds of fame, is of briefer duration, and leaves a man normally to live a longer time after his star has been eclipsed. Nebraska has enjoyed a decade of fame but now at thirty-one he hears the plaudits diminishing. Thus the professional baseball player's fame is waning before he reaches an age at which most men win fame.

Webber's fears for Nebraska, however, are groundless; the

Cherokee is made of firmer stuff than Jim Randolph. Wolfe wrote Arthur Mann that he wanted Nebraska to be "strong, simple, full of earth and sun," and in this aim he succeeded very well. Nebraska has prepared for his retirement by purchasing a farm and is looking forward with pleasure to living on his own land. Nebraska has remained singularly free from the allure of the "shining city," and despite his urban sojourn, he retains as his abiding values an appreciation of and love for the humblest American life —life on the land.

Wolfe's purpose in this idealized portrait of Nebraska is not just to portray a wholesome and incorruptible American whom success and fame cannot spoil. Nebraska becomes the symbol of the primary qualities of America, the very antithesis of all the evils which Wolfe condemns in "Boom Town." Traveling on the same train with Webber and Crane are the boom-minded and money-mad speculators who are also the leaders of Libya Hill: Mayor Baxter Kennedy, Jarvis Riggs the banker, and Parson Flack the political manipulator, all of whom the terrible Judge Bland calls "As eminent a set of sons-of-bitches as were ever gathered together in the narrow confines of a single pullman car." These bitter words of the blind lawyer echo the sentiments of Wolfe, and Nebraska the peerless stands in spotless contrast to the tainted souls of this group. As Webber, after his return from Europe, had turned to Nebraska the ballplayer to "get back in his blood once more the honest tang of America," so Wolfe turns to Nebraska the Zebulon farmer as the symbol of the positive values of America, and in so doing creates a character more typical of Jeffersonian nineteenth-century idealistic agrarianism than of the regional revolt of the Nashville agrarians during the Roaring Twenties.[9]

The idealization of Nebraska as a representative American tends at times to obscure his Indian blood, but Wolfe does portray Nebraska as having a much deeper Indian heritage than that which accounts for the color of his hair, eyes, and skin—though he emphasizes different aspects of this racial heritage in the youth and the mature man. In Nebraska the youth this deeper racial inheritance is buried within the personality but when it comes to the surface, as it does on occasion, Nebraska exhibits his kinship to the "wild and barbarous race." When Nebraska defended George Webber, the hand that swung the baseball bat was the hand that swung the tomahawk—only the weapon is different.

The chief Indian trait which Wolfe emphasizes in Nebraska the mature man is fatalism. It is not, however, a metaphysical fatalism such as Spinoza and Hegel wrought into systems, nor is it a mystical religious fatalism which in Christianity produced predestination and in Mohammedanism resulted in kismet. In Nebraska it is the fatalism of the aborigine, the simple acceptance of things as they are. Hence Nebraska's fortitude and his serene acceptance of the ups and downs of life—a quality Webber obviously envies —are attributed by Wolfe to Nebraska's Indian heritage.

When the posthumous publication of *The Web and the Rock* and *You Can't Go Home Again* added Nebraska to the Wolfe gallery, they also precipitated a search for Nebraska's prototype. Knowing Wolfe's usual methods of characterization, his readers combed the rosters of the major leagues and the sport pages of Asheville newspaper files in vain efforts to find the model for Nebraska. Edward C. Aswell, writing before the publication of Wolfe's letters, stated flatly that there was no prototype for Nebraska, and used Nebraska as "a perfect example of free invention" to defend Wolfe against the charge of "autobiographical writer." But the publication of Wolfe's letters in 1956 reopened the question of Nebraska's prototype. In his letter to Arthur Mann Wolfe writes of Nebraska: "I have got the man, I knew him as a child—he never made the Big League, but he could have." And the first accurate identification of Nebraska's main prototype occurred when Richard S. Kennedy published his monumental study of Wolfe's literary career in 1962: "Wolfe's remark in a letter to Arthur Mann probably refers to Max Israel." [10] In naming Max Israel as the principle prototype of Nebraska Crane, Mr. Kennedy is certainly correct, though there were others too.

Max Israel appears in *Look Homeward, Angel* as Max Isaacs, Eugene's childhood friend. As the novel progresses the importance of Max diminishes and he does not appear after Eugene's trip to Charleston, when he was one of the group who made the trip. After Eugene entered the Altamont Fitting School he made other friends, but though his friendship with Max waned, he was still interested in Max because of his baseball ability.

> Max Isaacs continued to interest him as an athlete long after he ceased to interest him as a person. The game Max Isaacs excelled in was baseball. Usually he played one of the outfield positions, ranging easily about in his field, when a ball was hit to him, with the speed of a panther, making impossible catches with effortless grace. He was a terrific hitter, standing at the plate casually but alertly, and meeting the ball squarely with a level swinging smack of his heavy shoulders.[11]

Perhaps the reason Max has been overlooked as a prototype for Nebraska is that he was a blond—even to his eyebrows. Wolfe wrote of him in *Look Homeward, Angel:* "His hair was thick, straight, the color of taffy. He had blond eyebrows. There was much kindness in him."

Why, then, is Nebraska an Indian? Despite the fact that he is a composite character, the answer lies in the deeper meaning of Wolfe's purpose or rather multipurpose in the characterization of Nebraska. Over and beyond his other purposes, as discussed above, Wolfe apparently intended Nebraska as the symbolic American and, as such, Nebraska becomes Wolfe's answer to Robert Penn Warren's challenge.

In 1935 Mr. Warren published an essay-review of *Of Time and the River* which includes incisive comments on Wolfe's ability as a novelist to select and control his material. He was especially critical of old Gant as a fatherland symbol.

> The leading symbol of the father, old Gant, gradually assumes another aspect, not purely personal; he becomes, in other words a kind of symbol of the fatherland, the source, the land of violence, drunkenness, fecundity, beauty, and vigour on which the hero occasionally reflects during his wanderings and to which in the end he returns. But this symbol is not the total expression of the idea, which is worked out more explicitly and at length. There are long series of cinematic flashes of "phases of American life": locomotive drivers, gangsters, pioneers, little towns with the squares deserted at night, evangelists, housewives, rich and suicidal young men, whores on subways, drunk college boys.[12]

But Mr. Warren also praised Wolfe and challenged him.

> Mr. Wolfe promises to write some historical novels, and they may well be crucial in the definition of his genius, because he may be required to re-order the use of his powers. What, thus far, he has produced are fine fragments, several brilliant pieces of portraiture, and many sharp observations on men and nature: in other words, these books are really voluminous notes from which a fine novel, or several fine novels, might be written.

Though Wolfe did not like some of Mr. Warren's comments, the challenge did not go unanswered. Wolfe later came to know Warren well and to respect him. They were both on the program at the Colorado Writers' Conference the following summer, and Wolfe spent a pleasant evening with Warren in 1936.[13]

Wolfe felt that one of the distinguishing features of American life is a fundamental element of savagery. Though his diction is sometimes tricky, when his work is studied *in toto* it becomes evident that his conception of "savage" is not as a noun, but as an adjective whose connotation is best expressed by an aggregation of synonyms: fierce, ferocious, wild, cruel, barbarous. The result of this inherent savageness is often violence—another distinguishing feature of American life, according to Wolfe, and in his panoramic view he endeavors to demonstrate the presence of savagery. Although numerous examples can be cited, a few will suffice for illustration. In *Of Time and the River* he writes an extended paean to America which he maintains is "a fabulous country, the only fabulous country" but one that also has its shortcomings: "It is the place of violence and sudden death" and "the place that is savage and cruel." Even the loneliness which George Webber feels as "he walked the furious streets of life" is a "savage loneliness." And when Mark Joyner discourses on the faults of the Joyners he condemns their "Cruelty, blind indifference to everything except oneself, brutal neglect," and allowing their unwanted children to wage a "struggle to survive as barbarously savage as the children of an Indian tribe endure." Not only does Wolfe include this element of savageness in his own kaleidoscopic portrayal but he calls on other writers to do likewise. In his conclusion to *The Story of a Novel* he expresses this belief.

> Out of the billion forms of America, out of the savage violence and the dense complexity of all its swarming life; from the unique and single substance of this land and life of ours, must we draw the power and energy of our own life, the articulation of our speech, the substance of our art.[14]

If Wolfe ever created a studied "symbol of the fatherland" that symbol is not Eugene Gant or George Webber or old Gant; that symbol is Nebraska Crane. Mr. Warren's choice of the word "fatherland" is propitious. The Germanophile soul of Thomas Wolfe ever clung to America as fatherland and more specifically to North Carolina, of which he wrote in masculine terms:

> . . . the land has a brooding presence that is immensely old and masculine, its spirit is rugged and desolate, yet it broods over its people with stern benevolence. The earth is a woman, but Old Catawba is a man. The earth is our mother and our nurse, and we can know her, but Old Catawba is our father, and although we know that he is there, we shall never find him. He is there in the wilderness, and his brows are bowed with granite: he sees our lives and deaths and his stern compassion broods above us. Women love him, but only man can know him: only men who have cried out in their agony and their loneliness to their father, only men who have sought throughout the world to find him, can know Catawba: but this includes all the men who ever lived.[15]

The symbol for such a fatherland would have to be not only a man but a stalwart one at that, and preferably one who is also "bowed with granite." But to be a symbol of the entire fatherland, he must also include the fundamental savagery that is an integral part of America. How could this necessity be better met than by including in his veins the blood of the "wild and barbarous race"? And what blood could possibly be better for this purpose than Old Catawba's own Cherokees? Wolfe's deeper purpose in making Nebraska Crane a symbol of America, it seems to me, best explains his Indian blood. Thus in a sense Aswell was right when he wrote of Nebraska, "Tom created him." In drawing the lineaments of Nebraska, Wolfe certainly put more into him than the youthful Eugene found in Nebraska's principal prototype.

Nebraska Crane underwent a long process of development in Wolfe's mind which illustrates the increasingly free play that Wolfe allowed his imagination in his later writing. Although he continued to rely on real people as models, he made Nebraska a synthesis of more individual personalities than any character he ever created, and he also gave him many attributes that were not present in any of the prototypes. Consequently, Nebraska is the most composite characterization of all Wolfe's figures, and it hardly comes as a surprise that his development spanned Wolfe's entire career of fiction writing.

The character who eventually became Nebraska Crane first appears in a brief sketch in the holograph manuscript of "O Lost" as "Joe Redmond, paper boy," who comes to Perry's blacksmith shop to collect.[16] Joe Redmond did not make the final version of *Look Homeward, Angel* but Wolfe did not discard him. In 1930 he had been given the nickname "Goat" and Wolfe intended him for the ill-fated "The October Fair" as one of the boyhood friends of Monkey Hawke.[17] Two years later Goat Redmond was ticketed to be one of the passengers on "K 19" before it was derailed.[18] These two abortive attempts to use Goat Redmond only resulted in the further development of the character. By 1935 he had been rechristened Nebraska Redmond and he began to show some of his definitive lineaments.

In his speech to the University of Colorado Writers' Conference on August 6, 1935, Wolfe gave his audience a brief preview of Nebraska. This reference does not appear in *The Story of a Novel* because it was one of the passages Miss Nowell deleted from Wolfe's speech in editing it for publication. On page 45 of the published version the first paragraph ends with "the pretty girl who cracked the whip and thrust her head into the lion's mouth with Johnny J. Jones Carnival and Combined Shows." The following paragraph begins "Where now?" However, in his speech following the account of the daring miss of the Johnny J. Jones Carnival, Wolfe mentioned four other people: Mr. Hoffman, the "stonecutter who worked for my father and told fabulous stories"; a Negro driver for the Carolina Coal and Ice Company; "a boy named Victor Roncey" whom he disliked; and one whom he admired, Nebraska Redmond.

> . . . another boy named Nebraska Redmond who was a wonderful boy, a plain, gentle, countrified kind of boy as brave as a lion and good at everything—hunting, swimming, wrestling, playing baseball—and for that reason, I felt, so much like his wonderful name, Nebraska, that I could never think of him as possibly having any other name.[19]

In this brief sketch Nebraska's baseball ability is listed last among his talents, and Wolfe does not make any mention of Indian blood.

At various stages of his continued development Nebraska was given two other surnames besides Crane and Redmond. These were Crawford and Drake. Scattered among Wolfe's holograph manuscripts, variant versions, pocket notebooks, and notes are many references to and sketches of Nebraska coupled with one or another of his four surnames. This practice of Wolfe's in giving various surnames to a character is by no means unique in Nebraska's case, as he frequently tried several names for a character before he reached a final decision. Esther Jack, for example, was also called Rebecca Feitlebaum and Esther Jacobs in earlier stages of her development before Wolfe selected the symbolic surname Jack in mid-1937. In the case of Nebraska, however, it is fortunate that Wolfe kept changing his surname because by examining the references to the several names it is possible to determine the additional evolution which Nebraska underwent before he emerged as Nebraska Crane.

The second choice of a surname for Nebraska was Crawford. In a draft employing this surname he takes on other attributes that are characteristic of Nebraska Crane.

> Nebraska Crawford was a fellow that I liked. That was a queer name sure enough, but there was also something good about it. It was a square, thick, muscular, brawny, browned and freckled, wholesome kind of name, plain as an old shoe and afraid of nothing and yet it had some strangeness in it, too. And that was the kind of a boy Nebraska Crawford was. He was a poor boy, and

lived out in "the Doubleday section," which was a tough part of town.[20]

In discussing Nebraska's name here Wolfe does not say that it is Indian; he simply says that "it had some strangeness in it." It was not until later that he accounted for this "strangeness" by attributing Indian blood to Nebraska. Evidently Wolfe felt that Crawford was not an appropriate name for one with Indian blood, for in manuscripts where references to Nebraska's Indian blood begin to appear the name Crawford is also discarded.

After abandoning Crawford, Wolfe began to use Drake as Nebraska's surname. Although he employed the name Crawford in manuscripts where the autobiographical protagonist is George Josiah Spangler, he had his typist go back and rename the character Drake. In a version of the rescue scene, where Spangler is defended by Nebraska Crawford, Crawford is marked out and Drake is typed in.[21] Nebraska's father is introduced into this same manuscript as Jim Drake. By this time Wolfe had decided to give Nebraska Indian blood, and in this section most of the Cherokee references are made to Nebraska Drake which occur in the published account of Nebraska Crane. On page thirty-seven of the manuscript Wolfe crossed out Drake with his pencil and wrote above it Crane. Nebraska's definitive surname had at last been chosen.

After Nebraska's final name was selected, however, he continued to undergo change and development. When Wolfe decided to make Nebraska George Webber's best friend he moved him from "the Doubleday section" on the west side of town and established him across the street from Mark Joyner's (Webber's uncle's) home. This action explains the statement in *The Web and the Rock:* "Nebraska Crane and his family were recent-comers to this part of town. Formerly, he had lived out in 'the Doubleday Section.'" But more pertinent to this study is the fact that as Wolfe continued to write about Nebraska, he increasingly accentuated the Indian qualities of Nebraska.

In "The People of the Street" where Wolfe projected the other members of the Crane family he included a summary of Nebraska as one of "The five boys of the Street."

> *Nebraska Crane,* the son of a policeman, a boy with coarse black hair, a square freckled face, and tar black eyes, is the best and bravest boy in town. He is afraid of nothing. He can do everything better than anyone else and can hit a baseball farther. He has a touch of Cherokee blood in him.[22]

This summary is indicative of the development of Nebraska as the symbolic figure he finally became. The emphasis here is on baseball and the Indian blood, though mentioned, is minimized. However, as Wolfe developed Nebraska further the "touch of Cherokee blood" increased in importance in ratio to Nebraska's symbolic implications.

On a yellow sheet Wolfe once jotted down his ideas about some of the characters on which he was then working and which he intended for his Joe Doaks book. Nebraska headed the list.

> Nebraska Crane: The man of nature.
> Alsop: The man of sentiment—"all things for the best."
> [Dexter] Joyner: The man of fashion—the eternal trifler is with us yet.
> Jim [Doaks, who became Randy Shepperton in *You Can't Go Home Again*]: The Conservative—"a man with both feet on the ground—That's . . . [sic] that's the American way of doing things." [23]

The characterization of Nebraska Crane was left unfinished by Wolfe's death,[24] but in bringing Nebraska's lineaments into clear focus Wolfe leaves no doubt about Nebraska's symbolic importance. As "the man of nature" he represents the qualities which Wolfe considered essentially good and fundamentally American. His Indian heritage carries with it a basic savagery which Wolfe also considered characteristically American. Thus in the final analysis it is Nebraska Crane rather than the introspective Eugene Gant or the socially conscious George Webber who approaches archetypal statue as the fitting symbol of the fatherland.

Nebraska is of mixed blood but one whose heritage includes that of the primeval inhabitants of the land which conveys a residual savagery that he controls and directs. His optimistic fatalism is a personal extension of the nineteenth century concept of Manifest Destiny, and his athletic career in the national sport epitomizes the fulfillment of the American dream, but he remains unspoiled and is impervious to the allure of fame. He is a provincial who resists the blandishments of the city and stays free from the corruptions of urban life. He is a lover of the land as a true agrarian and not as a speculator. He is Thomas Wolfe's *beau ideal* and therefore the appropriate symbol for his beloved America, "the only fabulous country . . . where miracles not only happen, but where they happen all the time."

6 The Achievement:

'The Memory of the Lost America' and 'Even the Least of These, Our Brothers'

In the twelve years he devoted to fiction writing Thomas Wolfe did not, of course, reach his goal of covering 150 years with the action of 2,000 characters who would include almost every racial type of American life, but his accomplishment is remarkable. He covered with thoroughness only about one-fifth of his projected time span, the first thirty-five years of the twentieth century, but in the number of characters he passed the half-way point; the pages of his six books and two full-length plays teem with 1,037 named characters and many others who are unnamed. His range in the presentation of race and nationality is no less impressive. The twenty nationalities he includes along with the Negro, Jew, and Indian comprise the racial and national origins of the vast majority of Americans.

The resulting picture which Wolfe gives of America, as seen through the eyes of his two autobiographical protagonists, is largely that of the first third of the twentieth century but the point of view is substantially that of the nineteenth. America's true greatness is implicitly attributed to its Anglo-Saxon derivation, and the real Americans are those wholly indigenous, especially those whose ancestors' axes and rifles helped to establish the nation in the wilderness. Americans whose assimilation is less than total, even though they may be native born, are viewed with distrust, and some groups in this category are branded as inherently inferior. The tendency of those whose acculturation is incomplete to cluster in urban centers subjects them to the false ideas of the city and further insulates them from the rural values whence came the spiritual strength of America. In short, the "old" Americans are distinctly superior and in every way preferable.

As an expression of the attitudes prevalent during Wolfe's boyhood this fictional view is an accurate one. His absorbent and retentive memory and his method of fictional fidelity in employing the cargo of that memory ensured a picture completely representative of his most impressionable years. But neither the nation nor the artist remained at that point of development. Some of the attitudes Wolfe portrays had already vanished from the national scene by the time he wrote and others were on the wane, so that his general picture reflects a bygone era and has become but the memory of an America lost under the myriad changes of the twentieth century.

Among these numerous changes one of the most significant occurred midway in Wolfe's lifetime—the transition from a rural to an urban nation. The population shifts during the First World War tipped the balance, and the census of 1920 was the first to show that city dwellers outnumbered rural America. The accompanying reassessment of the country's rural heritage resulted in ideas, mores, and values that contrast markedly with those of the preceding epoch, especially with regard to race and nationality. Wolfe, who left North Carolina in 1920 and spent the second half of his life in the urban East, was also undergoing change, though the evidence of change is not nearly so conspicuous in his fiction as is his reflection of the former era.

One of the several critical fallacies about Wolfe is to equate the Gant and Webber cycles completely and to consider the Webber cycle as simply a retelling of the Gant story with little significant change. But a careful reading of the latter will disclose that in addition to much repetition there are significant aspects of George Webber that are not visible in Eugene Gant. One of the most important differences between the two is Webber's growing expression of individual worth and the brotherhood of man, which makes him a harbinger of the ideal which has become paramount in the second half of the twentieth century.

Though Webber's early years are thoroughly Gantian, his story proceeds further than that of the egocentric Eugene, and the additional portion contains an entirely new attitude. *You Can't Go Home Again* begins with Webber in a reflective mood during which he candidly acknowledges that it has taken a long time for him to grow up. Among the things he has learned, however, is that he is "the son and brother of all men living," an identification

Eugene never makes. As if to emphasize that this new view is not just a flash of Wolfean rhetoric, the additional characterization of Webber includes some development of it. To Randy Shepperton's reminder that "New York is not America," George Webber replies "I know" and then goes on to complain that "the real things like freedom, and equal opportunity, and the integrity and worth of the individual" have become "just words." Not only is this new angle of vision true of Webber the man but it is also true of Webber the artist. Wolfe did not resist the temptation to have his writer-protagonists evaluate "their" earlier works, and just as Eugene Gant discusses *Mannerhouse* so does George consider his novel *Home to Our Mountains,* the most transparent disguise possible for *Look Homeward, Angel.* In discussing the "nameless wound" of America, Webber's point of view is enunciated unequivocally:

> We must look, and with our own eyes see, the central core of defeat and shame and failure which we have wrought in the lives of even the least of these, our brothers. And why must we look? Because we must probe to the bottom of our collective wound. As men, as Americans, we can no longer cringe away and lie. Are we not all warmed by the same sun, frozen by the same cold, shone on by the same lights of time and horror here in America? Yes, and if we do not look and see it, we shall be all damned together.[1]

Webber in spite of his prolonged growth has at last arrived at a point where his delayed maturity bespeaks a hard-won modernity. But his story was rapidly drawing to an abrupt ending, and this new note is largely drowned out by such earlier fulminations as the diatribes against Esther's people in *The Web and the Rock,* which in time of composition actually date from the same period that produced *Of Time and the River.*

The very fact that an emphasis on the brotherhood of man is diametrically opposite to the views expressed in his earlier writing and appears most clearly in *You Can't Go Home Again* may tend to make its genuineness suspect. The incomplete state of Wolfe's manuscripts at his death necessitated considerable editorial work before the posthumous volumes could be published, but not even the Harper's staff was aware of the extent to which Edward Aswell went in readying the books for the press. As Mr. Kennedy has shown, Aswell's hand is much heavier in *You Can't Go Home Again* than in *The Web and the Rock,* and he did not always resist the temptation to play the role of author as well as editor. The question could, therefore, legitimately be raised as to whether Webber's vibrant social concern and new point of view are the result of a change in the author or whether they were grafted—or at least accentuated—by an editor immune to auctorial review. But Aswell's revisions, for the most part, are stylistic, and the basic ideas Wolfe expressed remain unchanged. Webber's new outlook is not the result of any editorial shenanigan but a genuine change in his creator.

Undoubtedly the greatest single influence on the awakening of Wolfe's social concern was the Depression years he spent in Brooklyn, as he himself attests. It was the intense suffering that he witnessed which caused him "more and more to feel an intense and passionate concern for the interests and designs of my fellow men and of all humanity." This experience was supplemented by his observations of Nazi oppression in his beloved Germany in 1936. The man who ten years earlier had written "Drown a Jew and hit a nigger" now cheered so loudly for Jesse Owens at the Berlin Olympics that Hitler cast an angry glance at Wolfe, and Wolfe saw in a captured Jew the "image of a brother's face." After this trip he came home to write "The Child by Tiger" and "I Have a Thing to Tell You." These two stirring pieces and other writing he did in 1937 and 1938 indicate that he had at last become not only conscious of "the whole family of the earth" but that he realized that all men are members of the same great family and that race and nationality are but superficial distinctions which should not obliterate the essential kinship of mankind.

What Wolfe might have done had he lived or how far he would have pursued these new ideas in his fiction, no one can say. Any prediction beyond what he actually committed to paper would be but speculation, no matter how informed the guesser. One must recognize that the three posthumous books would be different had Wolfe lived to see them through the press. He had also reacted against other ideas that were prevalent when he grew up and had plans to work additional social protests into his fiction. His notes show, for example, that at the time of his death he was preparing to attack the overemphasis of utilitarian values in American life that the nineteenth century had bequeathed to the twentieth.[2] But while his notes, projections, and incomplete drafts point the direction in which he was working, most of them are too fragmentary for posthumous publication in his books, and Wolfe's final development can only be glimpsed in his published works.

Thomas Wolfe like George Webber reached maturity late, but the significant fact—and one frequently overlooked—is that he did achieve a maturity of social thinking as the center of his interest shifted near the end of his life from the individual to the society which shapes the individual. The egocentric preoccupation of the romantic rebel in Eugene Gant has made a much greater impact on Wolfe's readers than has the broadening and deepening humanitarianism of George Webber, though the latter is undeniably present, even though incompletely expressed, in Wolfe's fiction. This change in his principal protagonist parallels the one taking place in Wolfe himself, which in turn mirrors that of the nation's own gradual progress in the vast shift in viewpoint from nineteenth-century fetishism of externals to the twentieth's vigorous emphasis on individual worth.

Wolfe's approach to his writing was intuitive, however, rather than analytically logical, and the structure of his work is derived mainly from the ordering of his own experience. Since he was the child of his own times to an extent far greater than he himself realized, his intuitive rendition of personal experience became not only a romantic odyssey but also a vivid portrayal of his milieu. In his effort to capture "the whole web of America" he has given in his fictional treatment of race and nationality the historic attitudes toward this important aspect of American life during a pivotal era and has adumbrated the attendant struggle against inherited prejudice in the process of maturation. In this instance he comes near to realizing the generic American through the autobiographical self and to making his personal odyssey representative of the national odyssey.

Thomas Wolfe brought to his task impressive capabilities: immense talent, vast energy, colossal ambition; but in addition to these qualities (all essential for an epic writer) his assortment of prejudices was equally outsized and profoundly affected his writing for both good and ill. Seldom has subjectivity so dominated the work of an important author as is true of Wolfe's entire corpus. His personal feelings about race and nationality not only determined a great deal of the material he used but they also account for some of his power as a writer since his art comes squarely and often richly out of his very subjectivity. The tension that evolves from his ambivalent attitudes frequently provides the conflict that gives his fiction much of its interest. And the vividness of his characterization owes much to the intensity of his own emotions. Yet in spite of these positive factors, Wolfe's attitudes on race and nationality seriously flawed his work and constituted a major impediment to the attainment of his ultimate goal.

The desire to embody America in a work of art is by no means unique with Wolfe. Many writers have shared this epic impulse, but none has attempted to execute it on the scale of magnitude and complexity that Wolfe sought to achieve. William Faulkner concentrated on a single county, and Ellen Glasgow was content with the confines of one state, but Wolfe must capture the entire nation in his pages. This enormous purpose—the creation of the American epic—became his overriding aim and provided the motive force that drove him in his frantic and herculean effort.

The writer who seeks to transmute the essence of America into literary expression encounters all the artistic problems which have historically faced the creators of national epics in world literature plus additional difficulty. If the epic arises, as John Crowe Ransom has maintained, "as the expression of a nation which has gone through its strife," then any contemporary attempt to create an American epic is premature and faces extra hazard. Whereas the European writer in dealing with his own people is confronting a culture that has already acquired a basic unity and stability and for which he has a fundamental affinity, his American counterpart is granted no such artistic advantage. America, in spite of its illusory uniformity and its surface unity, is a nation still undergoing a struggle of contending racial and national cultures and remains a conglomeration of peoples rather than a cohesive people. The American epic writer is placed in a situation that not only demands insight into diverse components but also requires great empathy with elements for which he has little or no cultural affinity. If these demands are to be met by an autobiographical self then that self must be remarkably perspicacious and thoroughly egalitarian.

Wolfe fulfilled the first requirement well enough; it was the second that proved his artistic undoing. His panoramic portrayal of America's people caught their variety and vitality but lacks balance and objectivity. A vision clouded by prejudice and restricted by intolerance can only result in a twisted and partial picture. Since most of the time he viewed his fellow countrymen with a jaundiced eye indeed, it is not surprising that he frequently was more successful in recording the differences of various minority groups than he was in penetrating their true *ethos* or assessing their contributions to the American character.

But his total picture clearly reveals something else as well. Wolfe in time became aware of his prejudices and struggled manfully against them as a writer. He came to realize that in order to write a valid "story of the artist as a man who is derived out of the common family of earth and who knows all the anguish, error, and frustration that any man alive can know," the artist must first rid himself of the limitations imposed by prejudice and intolerance. The best evidence of the progress he was making in this direction is found in the emerging expression of the brotherhood of man in his late writing.

Although he had ability, dedication, and a genuine love for his country, Wolfe's effort to render the American experience into a prose epic is uneven, flawed, and in the final analysis a failure despite its heroic proportions. The main cause of this failure, though not the only one, is ironically the same source as that of much of his virtue as a writer—his complete absorption of American life. One of the main concepts that has dominated American life to the point of obsession is its concern with race and nationality. In his initial, uncritical acceptance of the attitudes of the majority of his countrymen, Wolfe acquired an artistic encumbrance that hindered him for most of his career. His views of race and nationality were the principal barrier to his achieving his avowed intent of probing "the whole consciousness of his people and nation." This was his burden, his albatross. But like the Ancient Mariner in his favorite poem, Wolfe too was eventually liberated. When his growth and advancement reached the point of his espousal of the brotherhood of man his albatross fell away.

This release came at the end of Wolfe's life when his work was not finished but simply ended. While it was too late to alter the fictional portrait he had already drawn, his renewed vision inspired a belief that his progress as an individual would be matched by his country as a whole. A declaration of his unswerving faith in America's progress toward the realization of its ideal became his valedictory.

> I believe that we are lost here in America, but I believe we shall be found. And this belief, which mounts now to the catharsis of knowledge and conviction, is for me—and I think for all of us—not only our own hope, but America's everlasting, living dream. I think the life which we have fashioned in America, and which has fashioned us—the forms we made, the cells that grew, the honeycomb that was created—was self-destructive in its nature, and must be destroyed. I think these forms are dying and must die, just as I know that America and the people in it are deathless, undiscovered, and immortal, and must live.
>
> I think the true discovery of America is before us. I think the true fulfillment of our spirit, of our people, of our mighty and immortal land, is yet to come. I think the true discovery of our own democracy is still before us. And I think that all these things are certain as the morning, as inevitable as noon.[3]

Notes

Chapter 1—THE TASK

1. HCL*46AM-7 (69), Pocket Notebook 2, November 1926—September 1927, one of thirty-five pocket notebooks, hereafter cited as PN. Items in the William B. Wisdom Collection in the Houghton Library are also cited by their Harvard College Library accession numbers.

2. PN 5, October 24—November 15, 1928.

3. New York, 1936, p. 53.

4. Letter from William Faulkner to Richard Walser, quoted in Richard Walser, ed., *The Enigma of Thomas Wolfe: Biographical and Critical Selections* (Cambridge, Mass., 1953), p. vii.

5. HCL*46AM-7 (23), "Passage to England," Second Installment, p. 1, holograph manuscript.

6. "The Past: Seen Like a Flash," p. 2. HCL*46AM-7 (65). Rejected passages from the posthumous novels.

7. *The Letters of Thomas Wolfe to His Mother*, ed. C. Hugh Holman and Sue Fields Ross (Chapel Hill, 1968), p. 162.

8. Mrs. Julia Wolfe also had several uncles who fought in the Confederate Army. W. O. Wolfe's brother, George Wolf, and his brother-in-law, Eli Lentz (husband of Sarah Ellen Wolf), both fought in the Union Army, and Lentz was killed at Gettysburg.

9. "The Old Red Irish," rejected passages from the posthumous novels.

10. In 1900, the year of Wolfe's birth, the population of Buncombe County was 44,288 people and only 505 were foreign born. See U. S. Bureau of the Census, *Twelfth Census of the United States: 1900, Population*, vol. I, pt. 2 (Washington, 1901), p. 773.

Chapter 2—THE NEGRO

1. HCL*53M-165 (34). This essay is written in ink on a single sheet of orange paper. It was one of the fifty-six Wolfe manuscripts found among the papers of John Skally Terry at Terry's death.

2. *Esquire,* XLVIII (October, 1957), 58–83.

3. HCL*46AM-7 (11), "Niggertown," A Play. Early manuscript drafts, in various stages of development, including notes for a four-act version. This is a holograph manuscript written in pencil on yellow sheets. Although one or more pages is apparently missing, Wolfe's defense of his title is both clear and illuminative of his attitude.

4. Monroe N. Work, ed., *Negro Year Book: An Annual Encyclopedia of the Negro 1921–1922* (Tuskegee Institute, Ala., 1922), p. 73.

5. In 1920 the total population of Asheville was 28,504, of whom 7,145 were Negro (Work, *Negro Year Book* 1921–22, p. 402). The Negro thus constitutes one-fourth of the population; in *Welcome to Our City* the proportion is slightly higher: of the thirty named characters, nine are Negro.

6. *Look Homeward, Angel* (New York, 1929), p. 136.

7. HCL*53M-165 (31), fragmentary essay on the South and Slavery. This manuscript was found among the papers of the late John Skally Terry in a package of manuscripts which Mrs. Julia Wolfe marked "some of this describes house and rooms at old 92 Woodfin Street."

8. HCL*46AM-7 (26), "O Lost," deleted passages, typescript, pp. 262–263.

9. HCL*46AM-7 (46), Box 2, *Of Time and the River,* unpublished passages.

10. The inferiority of the Negro is actually rendered *reductio ad absurdum* in Scene 9 of *Welcome to Our City* when Professor Hutchings states, "Offhand I am able to produce the works of five sociologists, six psychologists, and eight economists and historians, a total of nineteen, composing in all over ninety-five hundred pages of solidly-documented scientific, historic, and economic evidence, all tending to show that the Negro is racially, morally, intellectually and physically an inferior." But this display of pseudo-erudition is a part of the caricature of Hutchings and is not a serious attempt to refute the myth of inferiority. The generalization given remains correct.

11. "O Lost," deleted passages, no pagination.

12. *The Angry Decade* (New York, 1947), p. 152. A similar view is expressed by W. M. Frohock, *The Novel of Violence in America* (Dallas, 1950), p. 51.

13. *The Web and the Rock* (New York, 1939), p. 196.

14. HCL*46AM-7 (56), Box 3, *The Web and the Rock,* typed drafts. For the novel, however, Aswell cut this passage and the boaster remains anonymous: "He was a little ferret-faced man with a furtive and uneasy eye, a mongrel mouth, and wiry jaw muscles" (*The Web and the Rock,* p. 154).

15. *You Can't Go Home Again* (New York, 1940), p. 73.

16. *Ibid.,* p. 507.

17. Wolfe's original title was derived from Vachel Lindsay's poem "The Congo," the subtitle of which is "A Study of the Negro Race." The poem is composed of three parts: I. Their Basic Savagery, II. Their Irrepressible High Spirits, III. The Hope of Their Religion. Some of the ideas expressed by Lindsay, especially in Parts I and III, are echoed by Dick Prosser.

18. PN 15, August 1930—February 1931.

19. PN 20, March—October 1933.

20. Floyd C. Watkins' discussion of "The Child by Tiger" in *Thomas Wolfe's Characters* (Norman, Okla., 1957), pp. 102–109, is also based on this newspaper source.

21. Pages 692–693.

22. *Of Time and the River* (New York, 1935), p. 607.

23. Wolfe's memory is in error on this point. The newspaper account of Bailey's death says he had "made his home in Asheville for a number of years at 173 South Main Street" (*Asheville Citizen,* November 14, 1906, p. 1).

24. HCL*46AM-7 (25), Autobiographical Outline, Notebook No. 1.

25. I am obligated for this information to Miss Myra Champion, Curator of the Thomas Wolfe Collection, Pack Memorial Library, Asheville, North Carolina.

Chapter 3—THE JEW

1. *The Angry Decade*, p. 158.
2. Harry L. Golden, *Jewish Roots in the Carolinas: A Pattern of American Philo-Semitism* (Greensboro, N. C., 1955), p. 42.
3. Harold U. Ribalow, "Of Jews and Thomas Wolfe," *Chicago Jewish Forum*, XIII (Winter, 1954–1955), p. 93.
4. Pages 431–432.
5. "Margaret Proctor," holograph manuscript, pp. 18–19. Rejected passages from the posthumous novels.
6. Autobiographical Outline, Notebook No. 2.
7. "Passage to England," "2nd Installment," holograph manuscript, p. 3.
8. "Passage to England," "2nd Installment," holograph manuscript, pp. 11–27. This installment is dated in Wolfe's hand: "Sunday, October 26 [1924]."
9. For a fuller discussion of Mr. Rosen, including his prototype, see Paschal Reeves, "Thomas Wolfe: Notes on Three Characters," *Modern Fiction Studies*, XI (Autumn, 1965), pp. 275–278.
10. *The Web and the Rock*, p. 438.
11. *Ibid.*
12. *Our Mutual Friend*, The New Oxford Illustrated Dickens (London, 1952), Book 4, Chap. IX, p. 726.
13. *The Web and the Rock*, pp. 513–514.
14. Elizabeth Nowell, *Thomas Wolfe: A Biography* (New York, 1960), pp. 112–113. The ellipsis is Miss Nowell's.
15. *New York Times*, September 25, 1933, p. 15.
16. *The Letters of Thomas Wolfe*, ed. Elizabeth Nowell (New York, 1956), pp. 393–394. Hereafter cited as *Letters*.
17. "Morning," pp. 7–8. Rejected passages from the posthumous novels. A duplicate copy of this manuscript bears the notation in Wolfe's handwriting: "October Fair/Mr. Jacobs."
18. Rejected passages from the posthumous novels. On the first page in Wolfe's handwriting is the title "Jacobs' Dream." But this is crossed out and has written under it in Aswell's hand: "Jack Asleep." However, in his Rough Outline of his Last Book Wolfe lists this passage as "Morning: Jack Asleep." See Richard S. Kennedy, *The Window of Memory: The Literary Career of Thomas Wolfe* (Chapel Hill, 1962), p. 433.
19. Rejected passages from the posthumous novels.
20. "Ike Brown," pp. 86–87. Rejected passages from the posthumous novels.
21. PN 18, ca. January 1932 to August 1932.
22. Thomas Clark Pollock and Oscar Cargill, *Thomas Wolfe at Washington Square* (New York, 1954), p. 47.
23. *Ibid.*, p. 139.
24. *A Wayward Quest: The Autobiography of Theresa Helburn* (Boston, 1960), p. 331.
25. *You Can't Go Home Again*, p. 271.
26. Although Mrs. Bernstein was the model for Esther Jack, Mr. Cargill's wise observation should be remembered: Mrs. Bernstein was "altered in a variety of ways into Esther Jack." *Wolfe at Washington Square*, p. 41. Wolfe's creative imagination did change his characters so that, although still identifiable, they differ in various respects from his models.
27. Aline Bernstein, *The Journey Down* (New York, 1938). The novel ends with a vivid chapter, "The Willow Tree" (pp. 278–305), in which "she" describes her experiences in the hospital after an attempt at suicide.
28. Letter from Mrs. Bernstein to Elizabeth Nowell in 1950, quoted in Nowell, *Thomas Wolfe*, p. 99.

29. *The Web and the Rock,* p. 364.

30. *Anti-Semite and Jew,* trans. George J. Becker (New York, 1948), pp. 48–49; originally published as *Réflexions sur la Question Juivre* (Paris, 1946).

31. *Of Time and the River,* p. 480.

32. Martha Wolfenstein, "Two Types of Jewish Mothers," in Marshall Sklare, ed., *The Jews: Social Patterns of an American Group* (Glencoe, Ill., 1958), p. 525.

33. Written on the back flyleaf of PN 27, April—June, 1935.

34. Leo Gurko, *Heroes, Highbrows and the Popular Mind* (Indianapolis, 1953), p. 194.

35. PN 2, November 1926—September 1927.

36. *The Web and the Rock,* pp. 556–557.

37. *You Can't Go Home Again,* p. 508.

38. Maud Bodkin, *Archetypal Patterns in Poetry* (London, 1934), p. 162.

39. *You Can't Go Home Again,* p. 699.

40. *The Short Novels of Thomas Wolfe,* ed. C. Hugh Holman (New York, 1961), p. 278.

41. *Ibid.,* p. 236.

42. Autobiographical Outline, Notebook No. 1.

43. "Sunday, July 6," PN 14, May—August 1930.

44. PN 12, October 1929—January 1930, p. 145. (The pages of this notebook have printed numbers.) The note was made in January, 1930.

45. "Rouen June 3," PN 14, May—August 1930.

46. PN 12, October 1929—January 1930, p. 140. The note was made in January 1930.

47. Rejected passages from the posthumous novels. An eleven-page holograph manuscript written in pencil on yellow second sheets.

Chapter 4—The Foreigner

1. "Sat July 17 [1927]." PN 2, November 1926—September 1927.

2. Autobiographical Outline, Notebook No. 1.

3. Rejected passages from the posthumous novels.

4. "O Lost," deleted passages, p. 512.

5. *Ibid.,* p. 513.

6. *Ibid.,* p. 514.

7. Page 20.

8. "Characters: People of the Street," pp. 11–12. *The Web and the Rock,* typed drafts, Box 1.

9. The population of Asheville in 1910 was 18,762 and almost a third (5,359) was Negro. Of the 13,403 white residents 386 were foreign born and the largest single group of this number contained seventy-seven who were born in England. These statistics, and others in this chapter relating to the number of foreign born residents of Asheville, are taken from official census figures. U. S. Bureau of the Census, *Thirteenth Census of the United States: 1910, Population,* vol. III, Montana-Wyoming (Washington, 1913), p. 313. The 1910 census figures are chosen because they most accurately reflect the milieu of Wolfe in his formative years.

10. For a more detailed discussion of the Scotch see Paschal Reeves, "Thomas Wolfe and His Scottish Heritage," *Southern Folklore Quarterly,* XXVIII (June, 1964), 134–141.

11. "The Men of Old Catawba," *From Death to Morning* (New York, 1935), p. 201.

12. *Of Time and the River,* p. 163.

13. *The Hills Beyond* (New York, 1941), p. 143.

14. "The Old Red Irish," rejected passages from the posthumous novels.

15. I am obligated to Thomas J. Wilson, who studied under Major Cain, for bringing this probability to my attention.

16. "No More Rivers," p. 60. HCL*46AM-7 (66) , Box 1, Unpublished passages.

17. Kennedy, *The Window of Memory*, p. 8.

18. *You Can't Go Home Again*, p. 199.

19. The elevator man who perished in the actual fire of the Bernstein's apartment building, The Marguery at 270 Park Avenue, was William Cass, aged fifty. The *New York Times* gives no further biographical information about him (January 4, 1930, pp. 1–2) . Wolfe's depiction of Enborg as Norwegian-Irish is apparently the result of creative intent and does not result from prototypal biography. In his manuscript "The Fire: The Tunneled Rock" Wolfe calls the elevator man John Kinealey, but Kinealey is marked out and Enborg is written above in Wolfe's hand. HCL*46AM-7 (59) , *You Can't Go Home Again,* typed drafts, Box 3.

20. *From Death to Morning*, p. 58.

21. *Asheville Citizen,* July 17, 1916. The *Citizen* errs, however, in reporting his name as Captain John C. Lipe; his first name was James.

22. *From Death to Morning*, pp. 18–19.

23. *Of Time and the River*, pp. 535–536.

24. John Higham, *Strangers in the Land: Patterns of American Nativism 1860– 1925* (New Brunswick, N. J., 1955) , p. 272. Grant's book, *The Passing of the Great Race,* was first published in 1916 and new editions appeared in 1921 and 1923. His ideas enjoyed a considerable vogue during the twenties. The terms "Mediterraneans" and "Nordics" are self-explanatory. "The group usually termed 'Alpine' which is very broad-headed, has chestnut-brown or black hair, hazel-grey or brown eyes. The nose is inclined to be broad and is frequently concave. The stature is medium, about 5 feet 4½ inches, and the body is thick-set. The range of this type is from Russia to central France." Julian S. Huxley and A. C. Haddon, *We Europeans: A Survey of "Racial" Problems* (New York, 1936) , pp. 143–144.

25. "London Tower," *Asheville Citizen,* July 19, 1925.

26. *The Letters of Thomas Wolfe to His Mother,* pp. 49–50.

Chapter 5—The Indian

1. For an explanation of this choice see Paschal Reeves, "Thomas Wolfe's 'Old Catawba,' " *Names,* XI (December, 1963) , pp. 254–256.

2. *The Hills Beyond,* p. 207.

3. "Characters: People of the Street," p. 11. Typed drafts and notes for *The Web and the Rock.*

4. A Note on Thomas Wolfe, *The Hills Beyond,* p. 358.

5. Pages 32–33.

6. I am obligated for this information to Thomas J. Wilson. Mr. Wilson was on the staff of the *Tar Heel* during Wolfe's editorship and he frequently pitched horseshoes with Wolfe during the school year 1919–1920.

7. Elsewhere Wolfe makes Nebraska a member of the Asheville team of the same league. The earliest manuscript of "An Introduction by a Friend" does not mention Nebraska Crane but Wolfe has written in the margin about Nebraska as a member of the "local" ball club which was stranded in Knoxville when the club manager took off with the cash. Rejected passages from the posthumous novels.

8. A five-page manuscript written in pencil on yellow sheets. HCL*46AM-7 (55) , Box 1, *The Web and the Rock,* manuscript drafts.

9. The agrarianism which Wolfe praises here is not to be confused with that espoused by the Nashville Agrarians who issued *I'll Take My Stand.* Wolfe roundly condemns the Nashville group in *The Web and the Rock* (pp. 242–243) as "the young gentlemen of the New Confederacy" who comprise an "aesthetic clique" and who know nothing of the soil; he dismisses them as just "lily-handed intellectuals of a Southern university." Neither does the creation of Nebraska in the agrarian tradition violate his Cherokee heritage. "The Cherokees were the most

'civilized' of Indians, patently an agrarian people, settled, on their way to learning and literacy, hard-working and brave" (Roy Harvey Pearce, *The Savages of America: A Study of the Indian and the Idea of Civilization* [Baltimore, 1953], p. 64).

10. Kennedy, *The Window of Memory*, p. 310, n. 19.

11. *Look Homeward, Angel*, p. 203. The rescue scene where Nebraska defends George Webber (*The Web and the Rock*, p. 39) may have had a counterpart in actuality when Max Israel defended Tom Wolfe. In his Autobiographical Outline Wolfe recalled, "When I got caught with Max in Niggertown—the two murderous black boys—" Notebook No. 1. He does not further elaborate the incident, but in any threatening situation the muscular Max would have been a good boy to have along. Later Wolfe wrote, "What is there to fear on earth if Nebraska Crane is there?" (*The Web and the Rock*, p. 63).

12. "A Note on the Hamlet of Thomas Wolfe," *American Review*, V (May, 1935), 203–204. (This essay is reprinted as "The Hamlet of Thomas Wolfe" in *The Enigma of Thomas Wolfe*, pp. 120–132.)

13. "On my trip South after Christmas I stopped off at Richmond and had not been there a day before I ran into Red Warren, Allen Tate, Caroline Gordon, John Crowe Ransom and many others who were there for a meeting of The Modern Language Association, I think. I spent a very pleasant evening with the Warrens, the Tates, the Brooks and Mr. Ransom. In fact I did almost everything except become a Southern Agrarian" (*Letters*, p. 615). Mr. Warren, however, does not recall ever discussing the Indian as a fatherland symbol with Wolfe in any of the conversations he had with him. Letter from Robert Penn Warren to Paschal Reeves, dated September 8, 1963.

14. Pages 92–93.

15. *From Death to Morning*, p. 187.

16. HCL MS 326F, "O Lost" holograph manuscript, ledger 13, pp. 468–496.

17. HCL*46AM-7 (30), "The October Fair," ledger 2, p. 262.

18. HCL*46AM-7 (30), "K 19" ledger.

19. Page 36 of a carbon copy of Wolfe's lecture showing Elizabeth Nowell's cutting for publication as *The Story of a Novel*. HCL*46AM-7 (30), a seventy-four page typed manuscript. Wolfe took the name from an elementary classmate at the Orange Street School, Nebraska Carlisle Redman, and made only a slight change—Redman became Redmond.

20. HCL*46AM-7 (56). *The Web and the Rock*, typed drafts. On the top of this section Wolfe wrote in pencil, "5 Nebraska and Names of Boys." This sketch, except for the last sentence, appears in *The Web and the Rock*, p. 47, though the surname is changed to Crane.

21. *Ibid.*, p. 20.

22. *The Web and the Rock*, typed drafts.

23. HCL*46AM-7 (61), Notes and Sketches for the posthumous books, including random remarks.

24. In the notebook which Wolfe used in the spring before his death he was still jotting down ideas about Nebraska: "Nebraska Crane was the best boy in town but _____ was poor white trash and a common louse." PN 33, Spring 1938—April 24–25, 1938. In *The Web and the Rock* this statement is: "Nebraska Crane was the best boy in town, but Sid Purtle was poor white trash and a mountain grill" (p. 43).

Chapter 6—The Achievement

1. *You Can't Go Home Again*, pp. 328–329.

2. For Wolfe's list of beliefs that were held by the people of Altamont in 1916 see Kennedy, *The Window of Memory*, p. 31.

3. *You Can't Go Home Again*, p. 741.

Selected
Bibliography

I. Works of Thomas Wolfe

A. *Unpublished Material*

(Items in the William B. Wisdom Collection in the Houghton Library are listed with their Harvard College Library accession numbers.)

HCL*46AM-7 (11). "Niggertown," a Play. Early manuscript drafts, in various stages of development, including notes for a four-act version, 1922–1923.

HCL*46AM-7 (12). "Niggertown," a Play in ten scenes. Two or more typescripts (mostly carbon copies). These include complete versions of all scenes except Scene 9, with several duplicate or variant scenes or fragments, with many revisions in the author's hand, 1923.

HCL*46AM-7 (23). "Passage to England," and other stories. Introduction and 1st Installment in typescript; Installments 2–8 and 11 are holograph manuscripts. Manuscript drafts, fragments, unidentified scraps, 1924–1925.

HCL*46AM-7 (25). Autobiographical Outline in preparation for "O Lost." Covering approximately the first twenty-five years of Wolfe's life, contained in two dissimilar notebooks, 1926.

   (1) Notebook No. 1. A French pad, 89 leaves, goes into 1916, last year at Roberts' school.

   (2) Notebook No. 2. An English notebook, 135 leaves, begins with "Cont 1916."

HCL MS 326F. Holograph manuscript of "O Lost," seventeen ledgers, 1926–1928.

HCL*46AM-7 (26). Deleted passages from "O Lost." Typescript with author's penciled revisions of some (not all) passages deleted before publication as *Look Homeward, Angel*. These pages are from the same typing as the complete typescript (HCL*46AM-156F) and agree in pagination, 1926–1928.

HCL*46AM-7 (30). Notes, outlines, sketches, episodes, and drafts for "The October Fair," fifteen volumes, 1928–1931.

HCL*46AM-7 (46). Unpublished passages from *Of Time and the River*. Typed drafts, including variants and duplicates, with extensive penciled revisions in Wolfe's hand, 1930–1934.

HCL*46AM-7 (50). Manuscripts and typescripts of *The Story of a Novel*, 1935–1936.

HCL*46AM-7 (55). Manuscript drafts of *The Web and the Rock*, chiefly the scenes after meeting Esther, including variants of some episodes, 1931–1937.

HCL*46AM-7 (56). Typescript drafts of *The Web and the Rock*, including variant versions and duplicates, some with extensive penciled revisions in Wolfe's hand, 1931–1937.

HCL*46AM-7 (58). Manuscript drafts, fragments, and notes for *You Can't Go Home Again*, 1936–1937.

HCL*46AM-7 (59). Typescript drafts for *You Can't Go Home Again*, including variant versions and duplicates, some with extensive penciled revisions in Wolfe's hand, 1936–1937.

HCL*46AM-7 (61). Notes and sketches for the posthumous books, including random remarks, 1937–1938.

HCL*46AM-7 (65). Rejected passages from the posthumous novels. Eighty-one passages (seventy-seven typescript, four holograph) separated into three arbitrary parts, 1930–1937.

HCL*46AM-7 (66). Miscellaneous manuscripts and typescripts, including many duplicates, of sixteen passages that are unpublished, 1930–1937.

HCL*46AM-7 (69). Thirty-five pocket notebooks, 1926–1938.

HCL*46AM-13. Thomas Wolfe's letters to Aline Bernstein, 1926–1931.

HCL*53M-165. Fifty-six Wolfe manuscripts found among the papers of John Skally Terry at his death. One dates from the Roberts' school, some are from the Chapel Hill years, and many are from the Harvard years, 1915–1937.

B. *Published Works*

"London Tower," *Asheville Citizen*, July 19, 1925.

Look Homeward, Angel. New York: Charles Scribner's Sons, 1929.

"The Web of Earth," *Scribner's Magazine*, XCII (July, 1932), 1–5, 43–64. Reprinted in *From Death to Morning*, pp. 212–304.

"Boom Town," *American Mercury*, XXXII (May, 1934), 21–39. Included in *You Can't Go Home Again*, pp. 88, 120, 140–146.

"The House of the Far and Lost," *Scribner's Magazine*, XCVI (August, 1934), 71–81. Included in *Of Time and the River*, pp. 619–627, 637–652.

"Dark in the Forest, Strange as Time," *Scribner's Magazine,* XCVI (November, 1934), 273–278. Reprinted in *From Death to Morning,* pp. 98–113.

"The Names of the Nation," *Modern Monthly,* VIII (December, 1934), 598–605. Included in *Of Time and the River,* pp. 861–870.

Of Time and the River. New York: Charles Scribner's Sons, 1935.

"Old Catawba," *Virginia Quarterly Review,* XI (April, 1935), 228–238. Included in *From Death to Morning,* pp. 185–187, 195–204.

"Polyphemus," *North American Review,* CCXL (June, 1935), 20–26. Included in *From Death to Morning,* pp. 187–195.

From Death to Morning. New York: Charles Scribner's Sons, 1935.

The Story of a Novel. New York: Charles Scribner's Sons, 1936.

"Fame and the Poet," *American Mercury,* XXXIX (October, 1936), 149–154.

"I Have a Thing to Tell You," *New Republic,* XC (March 10, 17, and 24, 1937), 132–136, 159–164, 202–207. Reprinted in *The Short Novels of Thomas Wolfe,* pp. 236–278.

"Mr. Malone," *New Yorker,* XIII (May 29, 1937), 22–27. Included in *The Web and the Rock,* pp. 526–536.

"'E, A Recollection," *New Yorker,* XIII (July 17, 1937), 22–26. Included in *You Can't Go Home Again,* pp. 513–527.

"The Child by Tiger," *Saturday Evening Post,* CCX (September 11, 1937), 10–11, 92–102. Included in *The Web and the Rock,* pp. 132–156.

The Web and the Rock. New York: Harper and Brothers, 1939.

You Can't Go Home Again. New York: Harper and Brothers, 1940.

The Hills Beyond. New York: Harper and Brothers, 1941.

Thomas Wolfe's Letters to His Mother, ed. John Skally Terry. New York: Charles Scribner's Sons, 1943.

Mannerhouse. New York: Harper and Brothers, 1948.

The Letters of Thomas Wolfe, ed. Elizabeth Nowell. New York: Charles Scribner's Sons, 1956.

"Welcome to Our City," *Esquire,* XLVIII (October, 1957), 58–83.

The Short Novels of Thomas Wolfe, ed. C. Hugh Holman. New York: Charles Scribner's Sons, 1961.

Thomas Wolfe's Purdue Speech: "Writing and Living," ed. William Braswell and Leslie A. Field. Lafayette, Ind.: Purdue University Studies, 1964.

The Letters of Thomas Wolfe to His Mother, ed. C. Hugh Holman and Sue Fields Ross. Chapel Hill: University of North Carolina Press, 1968.

II. OTHER WORKS

Adams, Agatha Boyd. *Thomas Wolfe: Carolina Student.* Chapel Hill: University of North Carolina Library, 1950.

Aldridge, John W., ed. *Critiques and Essays on Modern Fiction 1920–1951.* New York: Ronald Press Company, 1952.

Allen, Frederick Lewis. *Only Yesterday: An Informal History of the Nineteen-Twenties.* New York: Harper and Brothers, 1931.

The Alumni Review: The University of North Carolina. XIX (January, 1931).

Aswell, Edward C. "A Note on Thomas Wofe," in *The Hills Beyond,* pp. 351–386. New York: Harper and Brothers, 1941.

Barber, Philip W. "Tom Wolfe Writes a Play," *Harper's Magazine,* CCXVI (May, 1958), 71–76.

Beach, Joseph Warren. *American Fiction 1920–1940.* New York: Macmillan Company, 1941.

Bernstein, Aline. *An Actor's Daughter.* New York: Alfred A. Knopf, 1941.

———. *The Journey Down.* New York: Alfred A. Knopf, 1938.

———. *Three Blue Suits: Mr. Froelich, Herbert Wilson, Eugene.* New York: Equinox Cooperative Press, 1933.

Bernstein, Peretz F. *Jew-Hate as a Sociological Problem,* trans. David Saraph. New York: Philosophical Library, 1951.

Bodkin, Maud. *Archetypal Patterns in Poetry: Psychological Studies of Imagination.* London: Oxford University Press, 1934.

Bond, Frederick W. *The Negro and The Drama.* Washington: Associated Publishers, 1940.

Burke, W. J. and Will D. Howe. *American Books and Authors 1640–1940.* New York: Gramercy Publishing Company, 1943.

Cargill, Oscar and Thomas Clark Pollock, eds. *The Correspondence of Thomas Wolfe and Homer Andrew Watt.* New York: New York University Press, 1954.

Cash, W. J. *The Mind of the South.* New York: Alfred A. Knopf, 1941.

Clark, Edward. "Images of the Negro in the American Novel," *Jahrbuch für Amerikastudien,* V (1960), 175–184.

Dickens, Charles. *Our Mutual Friend.* The New Oxford Illustrated Dickens. London: Oxford University Press, 1952.

Fenton, Charles A. *The Apprenticeship of Ernest Hemingway: The Early Years.* New York: Farrar, Straus and Young, 1954.

Fiedler, Leslie A. "The Breakthrough: The American Jewish Novelist and the Fictional Image of the Jew," *Midstream,* IV (Winter, 1958), 15–35.

———. "Genesis: The American-Jewish Novel Through the Twenties," *Midstream,* IV (Summer, 1958), 21–33.

———. *Love and Death in the American Novel.* New York: Criterion Books, 1960.

Field, Leslie A., ed. *Thomas Wolfe: Three Decades of Criticism.* New York: New York University Press, 1968.

Fitzgerald, F. Scott. *The Letters of F. Scott Fitzgerald,* ed. Andrew Turnbull. New York: Charles Scribner's Sons, 1963.

Frohock, W. M. *The Novel of Violence in America: 1920–1950.* Dallas: Southern Methodist University Press, 1950.

Frye, Northrop. *Anatomy of Criticism.* Princeton: Princeton University Press, 1957.

Gardiner, Harold C., S. J., ed. *Fifty Years of the American Novel: A Christian Appraisal.* New York: Charles Scribner's Sons, 1951.

Geismar, Maxwell. *Writers in Crisis: The American Novel 1925–1940.* Boston: Houghton Mifflin Company, 1942.

Gelfant, Blanche Housman. *The American City Novel.* Norman: University of Oklahoma Press, 1954.

Golden, Harry L. *Jewish Roots in the Carolinas: A Pattern of American Philo-Semitism.* Greensboro, N. C.: Deal Printing Company, 1955.

Gray, Idyl Dial, ed. *Azure-Land: A Romance of the Mountains.* Asheville, N. C.: Advocate Publishing Company, 1924.

Gurko, Leo. *The Angry Decade.* New York: Dodd, Mead and Company, 1947.

———. *Heroes, Highbrows, and the Popular Mind.* Indianapolis: Bobbs-Merrill Company, 1953.

Helburn, Theresa. *A Wayward Quest: The Autobiography of Theresa Helburn.* Boston: Little, Brown and Company, 1960.

Higham, John. *Strangers in the Land: Patterns of American Nativism 1860–1925.* New Brunswick, N. J.: Rutgers University Press, 1955.

Hoffman, Frederick J. *The Twenties: American Writing in the Postwar Decade.* New York: Viking Press, 1955.

Holman, C. Hugh. "Thomas Wolfe: A Bibliographical Study," *Texas Studies in Literature and Language,* I (Autumn, 1959), 427–445.

Huxley, Julian S. and A. C. Haddon. *We Europeans: A Survey of "Racial" Problems.* New York: Harper and Brothers, 1936.

Johnson, Elmer D. *Of Time and Thomas Wolfe: A Bibliography with a Character Index of His Works.* New York: Scarecrow Press, 1959.

Keiser, Albert. *The Indian in American Literature.* New York: Oxford University Press, 1933.

Kennedy, Richard S. "Thomas Wolfe at Harvard, 1920–1923," *Harvard Library Bulletin,* IV (Autumn, 1950), 304–319.

———. *The Window of Memory: The Literary Career of Thomas Wolfe.* Chapel Hill: University of North Carolina Press, 1962.

Kennedy, William F. "Economic Ideas in Contemporary Literature— The Novels of Thomas Wolfe," *Southern Economics Journal,* XX (July, 1953), 35–50.

Langner, Lawrence. *The Magic Curtain: The Story of a Life in Two Fields, Theatre and Invention, by the Founder of the Theatre Guild.* New York: E. P. Dutton and Company, 1951.

Learsi, Rufus. *The Jews in America: A History.* Cleveland: World Publishing Company, 1954.

Loeb, Harold. *The Way it Was.* New York: Criterion Books, 1959.

Marden, Charles F. *Minorities in American Society.* New York: American Book Company, 1952.

Mersand, Joseph. *Traditions in American Literature: A Study of Jewish Characters and Authors.* New York: Modern Chapbooks, 1939.

Middlebrook, L. Ruth. "Reminiscences of Tom Wolfe," *American Mercury,* LXIII (November, 1946) , 544–549.

Modder, Montague Frank. *The Jew in the Literature of England to the End of the 19th Century.* Philadelphia: Jewish Publication Society of America, 1939.

Muller, Herbert J. *Thomas Wolfe.* Norfolk, Conn.: New Direction Books, 1947.

Neumann, Erich. *The Great Mother: An Analysis of the Archetype,* trans. Ralph Manheim. Bollingen Series, XLVII. New York: Pantheon Books, 1955.

Norwood, Hayden. *The Marble Man's Wife: Thomas Wolfe's Mother.* New York: Charles Scribner's Sons, 1947.

Nowell, Elizabeth. *Thomas Wolfe: A Biography.* New York: Doubleday and Company, 1960.

Pearce, Roy Harvey. *The Savages of America: A Study of the Indian and the Idea of Civilization.* Baltimore: Johns Hopkins Press, 1953.

[Perkins, Maxwell]. *Editor to Author: The Letters of Maxwell E. Perkins,* ed. John Hall Wheelock. New York: Charles Scribner's Sons, 1950.

Pollock, Thomas Clark and Oscar Cargill. *Thomas Wolfe at Washington Square.* New York: New York University Press, 1954.

Rahv, Philip. *Image and Idea: Fourteen Essays on Literary Themes.* Norfolk, Conn.: New Directions Books, 1949.

Reeves, George M., Jr. *Thomas Wolfe et L'Europe.* Paris: Jouve, 1955.

Reeves, Paschal. "The Humor of Thomas Wolfe," *Southern Folklore Quarterly,* XXIV (June, 1960) , 109–120.

———. "Thomas Wolfe's 'Old Catawba,' " *Names,* XI (December, 1963) , 254–256.

———. "Thomas Wolfe and His Scottish Heritage," *Southern Folklore Quarterly,* XXVIII (June, 1964) , 134–141.

———. "Thomas Wolfe on Publishers: Reaction to Rejection," *South Atlantic Quarterly,* LXIV (Summer, 1965) , 385–389.

———. "Thomas Wolfe: Notes on Three Characters," *Modern Fiction Studies,* XI (Autumn, 1965) , 275–285. Thomas Wolfe Special Number.

Ribalow, Harold U. "Of Jews and Thomas Wolfe," *Chicago Jewish Forum,* XIII (Winter, 1954–1955) , 89–99.

Rose, Arnold. *The Negro in America.* New York: Harper and Brothers, 1948.

Rubin, Louis D., Jr. *Thomas Wolfe: The Weather of His Youth.* Baton Rouge: Louisiana State University Press, 1955.

Russell, Mattie. "William Holland Thomas, White Chief of the North Carolina Cherokees." Unpublished Ph.D. dissertation, Duke University, 1956.

Sartre, Jean-Paul. *Anti-Semite and Jew,* trans. George J. Becker. New York: Schocken Books, 1948.

Schermerhorn, R. A. *These Our People: Minorities in American Culture*. Boston: D. C. Heath and Company, 1949.

Schorer, Mark. *Sinclair Lewis: An American Life*. New York: McGraw-Hill Book Company, 1961.

Simonson, Lee. *Part of a Lifetime: Drawings and Designs 1919–1940*. New York: Duell, Sloan and Pearce, 1943.

Sklare, Marshall, ed. *The Jews: Social Patterns of an American Group*. Glencoe, Ill.: The Free Press, 1958.

Spitz, Leon. "Was Wolfe an Anti-Semite?," *American Hebrew*, CLVIII (November 19, 1948), 5.

Starkey, Marion L. *The Cherokee Nation*. New York: Alfred A. Knopf, 1946.

Stern, Edith M. "A Man Who Was Unafraid," *Saturday Review of Literature*, XXIV (June 28, 1941), 10, 14.

Thompson, Edgar T., ed. *Race Relations and the Race Problem: A Definition and an Analysis*. Durham, N. C.: Duke University Press, 1939.

Turnbull, Andrew. *Thomas Wolfe*. New York: Charles Scribner's Sons, 1968.

U. S. Bureau of the Census. *Twelfth Census of the United States: 1900. Population*, I, pt. 2. Washington: United States Census Office, 1901.

———. *Thirteenth Census of the United States: 1910. Population*, III, Montana-Wyoming. Washington: Government Printing Office, 1913.

———. *Fifteenth Census of the United States: 1930. Population*, III, pt. 2, Montana-Wyoming. Washington: Government Printing Office, 1932.

Walser, Richard. *Thomas Wolfe: An Introduction and Interpretation*. New York: Barnes and Noble, 1961.

———, ed. *The Enigma of Thomas Wolfe: Biographical and Critical Selections*. Cambridge, Mass.: Harvard University Press, 1953.

Warren, Robert Penn. "A Note on the Hamlet of Thomas Wolfe," *American Review*, V (May, 1935), 191–208. Reprinted in Walser, *The Enigma of Thomas Wolfe*.

Watkins, Floyd C. "De Dry Bones in De Valley," *Southern Folklore Quarterly*, XX (June, 1956), 136–140.

———. *Thomas Wolfe's Characters: Portraits from Life*. Norman: University of Oklahoma Press, 1957.

Wellek, René and Austin Warren. *Theory of Literature*. New York: Harcourt, Brace and Company, 1949.

Wheaton, Mabel Wolfe with LeGette Blythe. *Thomas Wolfe and His Family*. Garden City, N. Y.: Doubleday and Company, 1961.

Who's Who in American Jewry, ed. John Simons. III (1938–1939). New York: National News Association, 1938.

Whyte, William Foote. *Street Corner Society: The Social Structure of an Italian Slum*, 2nd ed. Chicago: University of Chicago Press, 1955.

Wish, Harvey. *Society and Thought in Modern America: A Social and Intellectual History of the American People from 1865,* 2nd ed. New York: David McKay Company, 1962.

Work, Monroe N., ed. *Negro Year Book: An Annual Encyclopedia of the Negro 1921–1922.* Tuskegee Institute, Ala.: Negro Year Book Publishing Company, 1922.

Index

The names of characters in Wolfe's fiction are in capital letters. Wolfe's works are listed separately by title.